מסורה

ArtScroll Series®

Rabbi Nosson Scherman / Rabbi Meir Zlotowitz

General Editors

THE SUN

Parents relive
the War Years —
the struggle and the survival

Published by

Mesorah Publications, ltd

WILL RISE

by Miriam Dansky
based on a manuscript by E. Reifer

FIRST EDITION
First Impression ... March 2001

Published and Distributed by
MESORAH PUBLICATIONS, LTD.
4401 Second Avenue / Brooklyn, N.Y 11232

Distributed in Europe by
LEHMANNS
Unit E, Viking Industrial Park
Rolling Mill Road
Jarrow, Tyne & Wear, NE32 3DP
England

Distributed in Israel by
SIFRIATI / A. GITLER
6 Hayarkon Street
Bnei Brak 51127

Distributed in Australia and New Zealand by
GOLDS WORLD OF JUDAICA
3-13 William Street
Balaclava, Melbourne 3183
Victoria Australia

Distributed in South Africa by
KOLLEL BOOKSHOP
Shop 8A Norwood Hypermarket
Norwood 2196, Johannesburg, South Africa

Typography by CompuScribe at ArtScroll Studios, Ltd.

Printed in the United States of America by Noble Book Press Corp.
Bound by Sefercraft, Quality Bookbinders, Ltd., Brooklyn N.Y. 11232

Foreword

The Bluzhover Rebbe *zt"l* said that everyday every child (after studying the daily lessons prescribed by our Sages) should learn about the Holocaust, for it says in Deuteronomy 31:21: "It shall come to pass that when many evils and troubles are come upon them then this song shall testify before them as a witness." The tales of suffering and the testimonies — as told by Holocaust survivors — are a song, a hymn of praise, a testimony to the eternity of the Jewish people and the greatness of their spirit.

The story is told that in the midst of the blackness of the Holocaust, the Gestapo chief Kunda caught seventeen Gerrer *bochurim* with beards and *peyos* and brought them before Amon Goethe, *commandant* of the Plazow labor camp (where my in-laws were imprisoned).

"And who are these with the beards and sidelocks?" inquired Goethe.

"These are Talmudists," replied Kunda.

Goethe roared with laughter. "Talmudists! You mean they are not laborers. They have one half hour to finish their business."

One of the group, Yisroel Eisenberg, spoke up. He told his friends that this was a time to rejoice as they were about to die *al Kiddush Hashem*. To the complete amazement of the Germans, the boys, who were at the brink of death, began to dance and sing. And dancing still they leaped into the pit where they were cut down by a hail of bullets.

A kapo who was present testified that the Gestapo chief then approached the pit and mumbled, "These are angels, not people."

This was *Kiddush HaChaim* which facilitated *mesiras nefesh al Kiddush Hashem*.

The Klausenberger Rebbe *zt"l* said that the greatest miracle of all is that survivors of the Holocaust, after all they have witnessed and lived through, still believe and have faith in the A-mighty. This, he said, is the miracle of miracles, the greatest miracle ever to have taken place.

And this is the golden theme running through the heartrending wartime memories of my parents-in-law, so eloquently brought to life in the pages of this book. At first glance you could not have more disparate strands — a chassidic boy from Poland and a *frum* girl from an illustrious Hungarian Jewish family — different cultures, different backgrounds, different war experiences … and yet, how similar. Torn away from everything they knew and cherished, they clung stubbornly to their faith. And from the ashes they (as did my own parents, both concentration-camp survivors whose life-stories mirror those of my parents-in-law) determined to rebuild and replant the glorious family trees which had so viciously been cut down during the War.

For years their respective war memories had lain dormant, but remained still as painfully sharp and vivid to them as the day they occurred.

We continually urged them to record their experiences for posterity and they have now done so. We can in turn do no less than to carefully read and empathize with their sufferings and express the hope that in the *nachas* they derive from their children and future generations they will find some meaning to their survival.

Rosh Chodesh Nissan 5761
Hershel Frydenson
London

Table of Contents

Father's Story

Mother's Story

A Note to the Reader

Much of this book is the result of conversations between Avrohom Reifer and his parents, Shmuel and Edith Reifer, as well as their personal reflections and reminiscences.

To assist the reader, a single rule has been placed alongside those sections that are monologues and a double rule has been placed alongside the dialogues.

FATHER'S
STORY

Stories That Raise Questions

Stories were one commodity we were never short of during our childhood years. My father told stories, long, circuitous tales, of his childhood in Poland: the family timber yard, the cheder, the chassidic courts. My mother told of her childhood in Hungary: the grocery store in Sarospotok, the picturesque town surrounded by mountains and vineyards. We grew up absorbing these stories like sponges, so that they permeated our souls.

It was only much later that we realized that these represented more than fairy tales with which to tuck us into bed. This realization came with the growing knowledge that certain basics were mysteriously absent from our secure and loving childhood. If there was so much that seemed stolid and rooted, like our heavy bookcases, there was also something strangely missing. What was missing turned out really to be quite simple — grandparents, cousins, relatives of all shapes and sizes, the very people, or their offspring, who peopled these stories with their rampantly colorful personalities — in point of fact, the past. There was a gap, a hiatus, a disturbing lack of continuity, for my parents' stories never progressed beyond their childhood years. It all sounded so wonderfully cozy, warm and intense. It was as real to us as the colorful wallpaper of our nursery, and we carried this reality around with us every waking moment. What had happened to it all? Why were we in autumn-leaved London and not in father's Chrzanow, or mother's Sarospotok? We had the feeling that something vast and inexplicable had happened to dislodge and dislocate them, and our curiosity grew and grew. We agreed with one another that something awesome lay at the bottom of it all. There were certain tell-tale signs, certain glances that passed between my parents when they thought we weren't looking. We noticed other things too, such as my mother's inky blue-black tattoo on her forearm, which she never took pains to hide. Or my father, catching his breath sometimes, sucking in air as if there could never be enough for him.

How come, we reasoned, they told so much, so easily — and then simply stopped?

One day I dared to ask the inevitable question.

"Well, and where are they all now, these people?"

"Ah," my father said, assuming a look both dreamy and stern. "Now that's enough talk for one night. Please say 'Hamapil,' for you have to be up for school in the morning."

The lights were promptly switched off, and so was our line of questioning.

But then parents are sometimes strange. Who could say that our parents' strangeness was different than that of others? How were we to know that my parents belonged to that species, rare enough in England, called Holocaust survivors?

Holocaust Survivors

That knowledge came much later, and then only by degrees, in what I can but describe as a gradual dawning. It seemed to seep in around us in our early school years like something dense and cloudlike. Yet, once we knew it, we knew that we had always known it. It was that sort of 'knowing.' The gaps and crevices in my parents' storytelling were suddenly part of this huge, immeasurable 'black hole' of history. This, then, was what they had fallen into, sucked in with their childhoods indeed, their entire pasts — an abyss from which they had crawled and clawed their way back to normalcy. All **this**, including us, the comfortable house, the neighbors, the Englishness superimposed onto our personae — in short, the **present** — was 'this side.' And on the far shore, receding painfully inch by inch — was their 'other' world.

It was then that we began truly to feel their 'sadness.' Not that they were miserable or oppressive. No. They were, on the contrary, bright, convivial, ambitious, conscientious. In time, we came to realize that they were truly all these things — but **overly** so. It was as if nothing could ever again be casual for them. They simply had no time for a thoughtless remark, a lighthearted phrase, all those things which are the hallmark and the inalienable right of children.

One does not survive eight labor camps to fritter away one's life aimlessly. If one survives while everyone, literally **everyone** perishes, one carries around a sense of duty and purpose like a cup of precious liquid. In this connection, there is a story that springs to mind concerning a certain yeshivah student. He once asked a rabbi how to avoid unseeming thoughts which came to him when he should have been hard at work studying Gemara.

"My boy," the rabbi said kindly. "Go and get a wine goblet and fill it to the brim with liquid."

The boy thought this a little strange, but he complied.

"Now I want you to take a walk around town without spilling a drop."

The boy did this, but understandably with great difficulty. He then returned to the Torah sage.

"Well, tell me my boy," he said. "What did you see in town?"

"Nothing," the boy said. "I was so busy concentrating on not spilling the liquid that I kept my head down all the time."

"You have answered yourself," the Rabbi said. "If you will concentrate on your Torah learning with the same degree of *diligence, you will have no time for other distracting thoughts."*

This story presents us with an image of my parents. They walked around, or so it seemed to me as I grew older and understood more, head down, intent on not squandering a drop of that precious liquid we call daily living, and which we often, G-d forgive us, take for granted.

"Take a minute of it for granted?" their disappointed looks would seem almost accusatory. "For this I survived eight concentration camps? For this I survived Auschwitz, Kole, Blechhamer, the IG Farben Industrie, Gräditz, Faulbrück, Markstedt, Fünfteichen, Gerlitz, and finally Zittau where I was liberated?"

Imagine saying to my parents something as commonplace as, "I flunked my homework," or, "I got a bad mark in an exam."

And there it returned, unbidden like an over-familiar guest. The old accusation. "For this I survived —?" Did they say it out loud, or did we simply imagine them using this particular formula of words, words that hung in the air, as palpable as the threat of snow on a darkening December day?

Sorry mother, sorry father. Sorry, for rocking the boat, sorry for denting the carefully constructed façade of a liveable life into which you have invested no less than your youth, your tears, your lifeblood ...

But out on the street, where the air was free, I would shout at the wind, shout at the trees, at anyone who would listen:

Why does it have to matter so much? Why?

Why is so much invested in me? Why must I be their past, their present and the future all rolled into one?

*I **want** to be perhaps a little irresponsible! I want to fail exams, or bend the spines of my books!*

I want — oh, what do I want? Nothing more than this — not to have to carry their happiness carefully balanced in my upturned hands!

But wait, my dearest parents. Don't look so shocked, so alone, so hurt. Be strong again, and cheerfully ambitious. It's OK. I'll protect you from the coldness of the world outside. I'll live up to all your expectations. I will try harder, much harder. I promise.

Only do this one thing for me: Don't look sad.

Returning to the stories, it was at about the same time that we realized the huge potential of the word 'Shoah.' From the whispered murmurings of schoolmates, or smatterings gleaned from newspapers, we began to understand the symbolism of what we had called, up to now, 'dead end.'

"All their stories," I confided to my sister "come to a 'dead end.'"

Suddenly, we had an inkling why, one day, their world had simply stopped. At this, I began to imagine what would happen if our whole world as we knew it, were one day to simply 'cave in.' No more house, no more neighbors, no more school, and, of course, no more parents. In my dreams, it was just me and my very much younger sister, marooned in a world grown suddenly unrecognizable. What should we do? Where should we run? How to survive? And if all this happened to us, would we still be who we thought we were? Who or what would we be? Even a beggar possesses a past, and with it the freedom to return. We would own less than the beggar, who in all weathers sat in his tattered coat on the cold park bench in Clapton Common, throwing bread to the birds. How exactly had my parents survived? They must be endowed with some 'special power,' be somewhat superhuman. The 'why' and 'how' of their survival now began to haunt me day and night. We wondered, we surmised, we theorized; yet still we dared not step over the invisible dividing line that was their war experience. We had not heard their stories, the stories that mattered. For this, we would have to wait, with a terrible unassuaged longing for the truth.

Ten Years Later: A Momentous Moment

One day, my father turned to me and said, "Well, and how would you like to go to Poland?"

At the time, I was young and unattached.

"But why?"

"Your mother and I have discussed this matter carefully, as we always discuss all matters pertaining to your sister and yourself, and we have decided. I would like you to visit Chrzanow, like you to pray at the graves of my grandfather and great-grandfather. And when you marry, please G-d, and have children, to instruct them to do likewise. You will be able then to act as their guide. You will be able to tell them where to go."

Father was looking at me expectantly. He was by nature a reserved man, much given to a certain degree of introspection. Added to this, too, I think the way his experiences had shaped him, he was slightly detached from the society of men — a little wary, a little cynical of people's motives.

But here he was, casting me a look of unmistakable intensity.

I knew that this was a momentous moment, a watershed. So I took my chance.

"The answer is 'yes,' I will go to Poland."

He heaved an audible sigh of relief and sank back into his chair.

"But on one condition," I cautiously added.

"Condition?"

"Yes." By now my heart was pounding so loudly as to drown out both my words and his. It was like a giant pulse beating on ancient tribal drums.

"You recall your stories and those mother used to tell. Well, what I would like to know is —" I coughed and hemmed and hawed. "Exactly what happened after that?" I burst out at last.

Again, a sigh escaped him as old as the Jewish exile.

"Yes, I see," he said a little tiredly.

"We have tried, your mother and I, tried so hard to protect you from all that. There was no need to delve too much, you see. Too much pain, too much loss ..."

"But if I am to go, I would like to hear your stories first."

"That would be something," he nodded in slow assent.

"Something for posterity, too," I argued now a little wildly. "Like being able to show others after me the places where you lived."

"Lived and died," he corrected.

"Well, and you agree?"

It was uncharacteristic for me to be pressing my father in this way. I felt as if we had changed roles.

"Yes, yes, I suppose. The time has come for both of us to tell."

Hearing Their Stories

That is how it transpired that one autumn day I sat with a tape recorder between us, notepad and pencil at the ready, nervously tapping my fingers on the heavy mahogany table. It was a strange situation. In a way, I was eager to know. Yet, as I stood on the brink of knowing, I was gripped with a terrible fear. Perhaps it would be better to leave the ghosts of the past undisturbed, for with knowledge comes responsibility. The question was — was I ready to hear my parents' stories?

I had decided that I would listen to my father's story first. At some time during the process, I would travel to Poland. As my father began to tell his story, I was touched by the way in which he narrated it. I had known instinctively that father and mother would chose different ways of telling, in accordance with their different personalities. My father told me straightaway that he would prefer to tell his story in the third person, as though he

were the protagonist in a fictionalized account. I saw
immediately that this suited his dry objectivity, his slight cynical
stance, his ability to dissect character and motive. He would only
be able to cope with this emotion-laden journey into the past if he
would be able to distance himself in this way. But as his story
began to unfold, I found out more. He was blessed with an
exceptionally acute memory which had stored up hundreds of
details related to his experiences. And again, the sense of
detachment. Would one expect, for example, a young terrified
boy to remember the names and ranks of his oppressors?

But to return to where we were. We hovered at the brink for
a long time, coughing, letting the silence between us grow. Then
at last, he began at what he considered a critical point in his
story, his days in hiding in the attic of his grandfather's house.

These weeks of listening were for me the most taxing, for I
was living both in the past and in the present. Conversely, I
began to notice, along with the obvious pain in my father's
voice as he recounted his story, an emotion akin to relief. The
relief came, I suppose, at finally being able to speak — to speak
and record for posterity. This must be, I reflected, the ultimate
victory for every survivor. I am here. I live. I breathe. (This
much no survivor ever takes for granted.) I remember. I will
tell the world my story.

It required an inordinate amount of courage on both sides
— for him to speak and for me to listen.

This, in his own words, then, is my father's story.

We will begin Shmuel Reifer's story not exactly at the beginning, but at a point which marks perhaps, his nadir, his lowest, most alone point. The date is the 13th day of Adar I (February 18, 1943). The joyous spirit which is supposed to enter with the Purim months has long since deserted the streets of his hometown, Chrzanow. The young boy is in hiding in the loft of his grandfa-

Grandfather's house and Beis Midrash in Koscielecka, 1987

ther's house. This hiding place, along with myriads of others now operational in the ghettos of Poland, has been ingeniously constructed, attesting to the infinite nature of the human capacity for survival. In just such constrictive corners of the houses, in cellars or lofts, we find the Jews of Poland throughout the years of 1942 and 1943 collectively holding their breaths, as the terror on the streets draws blood-chillingly nearer, inch by inch. Here, pushed up, squeezed, cramped against friends, relatives, neighbors, children, unable to sit or lie, unable to stand with heads aloft, unable to cry out or stretch their limbs, there was little else to do but sit like rats waiting to be flushed out of sewers. The particular hiding place in which we find Shmuel Reifer cooped up all alone has been constructed out of a section of false ceiling. It is reached by means of a lightweight ladder, which is then withdrawn upwards into the loft itself, thereby concealing the hiding to all but the most astute or most persistent of observers. In this hiding place there was room to lie, or crouch, but not to stand. There were no toilet facilities; these would have to be used surreptitiously when all seemed quiet, in the top floor of his grandfather's house. However, this hiding place, Shmuel Reifer has said, was preferable to the one situated in the cellar of his own house.

Here, on this quiet evening, we find the youth alone. He has entered the hiding place, as was his custom, as night began to fall. Once he had clambered up the ladder and drawn it up behind him, he was locked in by others from the outside. His relatives would return to unlock the ceiling vault in the morning, but at least for these few hours he would get some sleep. He needed to conserve all his energies for the working hours of the day. But it was not to be. At some point during this night a noise began — which was at once unfamiliar, yet as deeply known to him as the skin on his own hand — not timorously, but as it always began, arrogantly, loudly, boldly. The megaphones announced in that peculiarly nasal Germanic sneer "Raus, raus ..." The Jews ostensibly sleeping in the surrounding houses knew that in the peculiar atmosphere of Poland of 1943, even a little sleep was begrudged them. To them it seemed that they could sink no lower than this, but in a few days, as so often in the past months, they would again be proved wrong, for most would soon be transported to an 'alien planet,' where even their right to draw breath would be systematically denied to them.

Shmuel Reifer, along with other Chrzanow inhabitants, awoke to the shouting and found that he had been shaken out of sleep into an ever-recurring nightmare. He half rose from his position on the bare boards and drew himself up a little by his hands. Despite the darkness he could see all that was now transpiring on the streets below. He could make out the shapes of headscarfed women drawing their coats together with one hand, the other tugging children, heads tousled in sleep, still clutching a beloved teddy bear or doll. Suitcases were being hauled along, their contents spilling onto the pavements. A low sound, not so much of shrieking, but of moaning, issued from the gathering crowd, a deep primeval groan of pain, centuries old, too deep to be borne. Above this, increasing in ferocity, he heard the barked commands in German, the occasional sounds of rifle shots, the deeper sounds of rifle butts striking flesh, being deployed indiscriminately against the pitiful human mass. All these were manifestations of the raging of a Germanic anger, too profound to be explained away in the usual terms of two sides in a conventional war. In that instant,

Shmuel knew he was witnessing, as he would later witness as a guest of eight different *lagers* constructed for his confinement by the Third Reich, nothing less than the embodiment of that old and fabled enemy of Israel, Amalek, mysteriously resurrected in the 20th century, here on the streets of his nondescript Polish hometown.

The boy was alone. He held his breath. This, too, was part of the ever-recurring nightmare, that he would be left here alone, while all the others were moved off to some unknown destination. He watched as the swelling crowd was herded into a large mass, still writhing, moaning as an animal in its last throes, but now essential-ly contained, manageable. Still he watched, holding his breath, as this human mass was shepherded down the main street and then led into the open marketplace. At night, this was a ghost square. Soon it filled up, as the crowd poured itself into every millimeter of space, every nook and cranny. Positioned high up as he was he could see all this occurring over the roofs of the houses. He witnessed the crowd's torturous walk to this open place, and their positioning themselves there according to the new contingency. Only the noises were becoming duller, less assailing, so that the events, as far as the boy was concerned, were already losing an edge of their sharpness. His hands still clutched the windowpane, his knuckles white. He had a foothold on a loose brick, which enabled him to lift himself a little higher. He let go and lowered himself to the ground again, and immediately his hands involuntarily flew to his cheeks. His finger-tips were wet, and he realized that he had been crying copious tears, only, such was the level of his fear at what he had just seen, that he had not been aware of it. He felt a sense of aloneness strike at his very bones. To all intents and purposes, he was the 'last survivor.' He may as well have been the lone human on an alien planet. Then, the thought struck him, a chilling one, and one perfectly attuned to his feelings. The door was locked from the outside. There was no one to release him from his self-inflicted prison, for had he not seen with his own eyes that they were all gone, swept away, sucked in to what apparently was a catastrophe of unprecedented proportions?

We leave our protagonist for the moment, waiting, shivering and alone in his hiding place. Dawn is breaking, streaking the sky with a pearly gray florescence. It is a day laden with the bite of winter in it, yet spring is fast approaching. We leave, too, the assembled mass of approximately three thousand Jews, sitting or crouching in Chrzanow's main square. The tears of the night have dried on their faces, and here is the sun rising weakly as on any other February morning. It seems unfair that this be so, that the laws of nature continue, as if unmoved by their plight. Well, and should the sun fail to rise, the sky fall in on the earth? There is a new resignation in their hearts, a new weariness, as they pass what may well be their last few hours on this earth in waiting. Oh! but such a waiting as this was we can hardly imagine! The very bricks of the buildings of Chrzanow's town square, the very cobblestones which also look on impassively, have surely never witnessed such a marketday as this, or such merchandise!

The exact workings of those strange, vast, barbed-wire cities, situated in the Polish forests, was not yet known with true preciseness. But what every Jew in Poland felt or sensed with some sixth sense was that this 'thing' which had been brewing steadily was somehow essentially different in magnitude than even the bloodiest pogrom which had checkered Polish Jewry's history, and could not be whistled away or waited out for all their protestations of compliance. No, it was something intensely evil which arose, and hung in the air, greeting every ghetto dweller anew each morning, even inhabiting their deeply troubled dreams.

Shmuel Reifer's Chzranow

Shmuel Reifer's birthplace, Chrzanow, was situated between Krakow and Katowice, in Upper Silesia. Its nationality was always contentious, for it had been a German town before 1918, but after the Great War, Poland claimed it as its own. It was a largish town of thirty-five thousand inhabitants, of which approximately one third were Jewish.

Chrzanow was close enough to Germany for the two to maintain trade links. This was a significant factor, especially for the Jews, who preferred to commute across the border to Germany, where they found it easier to make a living. The more liberal, forward-looking view of the Germans, as opposed to the Poles, facilitated this end, and was encapsulated in the well-known proverb: "*Leben und leben lassen* — Live and let live.*" In light of what was to ensue in the coming decades, this seemingly amiable saying would leave the bitterest taste. However, the truth was that there were simply more business opportunities to be had in industrialized Germany, as opposed to traditionally bigoted and more backward Poland. Thus, each week business dealings would keep some of Chrzanow's most respected householders in Germany from Sunday to Friday, and have them returning to Chrzanow well in time for candlelighting on Friday evenings. They spoke fluent Yiddish, and due to its similarity to German ensured that they would encounter few communication problems.

In point of fact, the assembly in the marketplace marked an 'ending,' or at least the beginning of the end, for the Jewish community of Chrzanow. What those shivering in the weak sun could not see was that this was only part of a vastly more infinite horror which would fester and exert its malignant influence up and down the length of this country, traditionally hostile to its Jewish guests, and ultimately across the breadth of the continent. When the arbiters of what passed for 'German justice' eventually emptied the Chrzanow houses of their inhabitants, they were effectively 'emptying' out centuries of Jewish tradition. For all the well-vaunted 'Jewish notion' of indispensability, they were 'dispensable' enough, as was amply demonstrated in the approving expressions of their gentile neighbors, clients, employees, schoolteachers, indeed the ordinary folk who lined the route to watch them being blown away forever from their 'shared history.'

Childhood

Shmuel Reifer dozed in his hideout. In truth there was little else for him to do, but half-lying, half sitting, to pass between sleep and consciousness, drifting idly from one state to another, as though he had all the time in the world. Indeed time was one commodity he may well have had, being in possession of little else but the clothes he had on. Once again, his mind traveled back to the time he was a boy of 11 or 12, opening his eyes in his narrow bedroom. Home was a nondescript apartment consisting of two rooms, a kitchen and toilet, but no bathroom. Let us not forget that until the late 1930's, running water in houses was virtually unknown. Of course, this necessitated the considerable trouble of fetching all water needed for domestic uses from a water pump, several streets away. Bathing was also a laborious business, with great kettles of water having to be boiled on the coal range. But somehow, all this activity added something distinctly 'homey' to the domestic atmosphere, which the hot and cold running water from the tap of later years can never quite

Moishe Dov Reifer

replicate. There were certain smells associated with specific activities, like washday or ironing day, which would linger in the memory, inextricably bound up with a simple, happy childhood, long after the occupants of these simple homes had been forced to vacate them. Shmuel Reifer would later encapsulate this sentiment in the words: "True, life then was simple, compared to that which we enjoy today. But nowadays, we live artificially, talk artificially, even look artificial."

On a typical day before the war, his time would be deployed in this manner. He would rise in pitch darkness at 5 a.m., make out the shape of his still-sleeping brother, Moishe, in the other bed, and vigorously shake him awake. It was not only dark in the narrow bedroom, but also freezing cold. Stamping his feet and blowing on his fingertips, he would open the curtains and peek outside. The *negel vasser* jug which lay on the floor would contain splinters of ice. Once dressed, he would hurry down the flight of stairs in the shadowy apartment building, and out onto the darkened pavement. Outside he would encounter one or two other boys, hurrying just as he was to *cheder*. There, the stove was already lit, the room half-filled with yawning youngsters. This image lingers in the mind as typical of pre-war Poland, round-faced boys, 'shtetl' caps pulled down firmly over their ears, poring over their Gemaras, their stern-faced teacher standing over them. It is after all the image of the renowned Yiddish song:

"Oifn pripechik brent a fierel
Un in shtieb is heis,
Un der 'rebbe' lerent kleine kinderlach,
Kometz aleph beis."

With a break only for morning prayers, the boys would continue to study until 1:30, at which time they would recess until 3. Resuming their afternoon studies, they would continue until 8, and, after supper, until 10 or 11 at night. Thus, the young Shmuel Reifer, in common with hundreds of others of his contemporaries, rarely saw the Chrzanow streets in daylight. At noon, the Chrzanow sun would peek its way in through the heavily barred windows, laying

Moishe Dov Reifer

a shaft of light across the cracked linoleum floor, the wooden, heavily indented desks, and the *rebbe's* fraying sleeve. It would settle on the page of Gemara in front of him, making the very letters dance a little, as he blinked shortsightedly, unaccustomed to the strong light.

Cheder was to be the only type of Jewish education the boy was destined to complete. This, together with the strength of mind and nerve amassed in the years to come, would have to suffice — to equip him to face the world beyond. Had the unimaginable not occurred, and this tight, securely knit world not been torn to shreds, no doubt he would have found his way to his father's sawmill. The mill had been in his family for generations. His father, grandfather, great-grandfather, each had earned his living there, preparing the logs, felled from the thick forests of Upper Silesia. The sawmill represented not just a livelihood, it was nothing less than a destiny. Here, the timbers would be carefully graded. The best, earmarked for furniture, would eventually find their way into the polished living rooms of the wealthy. The thinner, inferior boards would be set aside for humbler purposes, perhaps concluding their travels in the paper mills or coal mines of the industrial zones. In the coal mines the planks would be used to prop up the mine shafts. The timbers would be felled in winter, often in deep Polish snow. One severe Polish winter at the turn of the long century would perhaps have found Shmuel's great-grandfather, Elyakim Getzel Reifer, a commanding, bearded presence, supervising operations as stack after stack of logs arrived at the railroad station, having been transported the thirty-odd kilometers from the mill by horse-drawn sleigh.

Great-grandfather Elyakim Getzel Reifer's matzeivah in Chrzanow

Again, the boy in the attic opened his eyes, but it was still dark, although the frightful noises of the night had all but abated. How the 'night' swallows everything, he thought, even the unimaginable worst is swallowed up and silenced by that pervading blanket of darkness. Where had all the pain gone? It still existed, he knew, but had simply been moved a little way out of his orbit. And his pain, his aloneness, his cold, his fear? It existed too but where was it going? Towards what was it directed? He recalled a *midrash*, which he had studied in the *cheder* with the barred windows, about the *Shechinah* going into exile along with His chosen people. All the tears, the pleas, the cries of this long night were being collected into some kind of receptacle and stored lovingly and with infinite care so that not even one drop was lost. He formed a mental picture of his sister and brother, still waiting fearfully in a similar, more cramped hideout beneath their own apartment. It was as if they were frozen in time, like some black and white still-life images.

But, had the *Aktion* passed them by? He made a swift reckoning of streets, estimating the scale of the previous night's operation. He made his estimates according to the relative loudness of the megaphoned shouting: "Raus, raus." It was possible that it had just shaved by them beginning perhaps a street or two away. With this thought floating about him like some vague comforting cloud, he dozed again.

Shmuel Reifer's Grandparents

He was a boy of perhaps 4-and-a-half. He was sitting opposite his grandfather at the solid, mahogany dining table. Grandfather Reifer, who seemed to him a giant, almost mythical figure in his silken *kapote,* was urging him: "My Shmuelke, you're not concentrating. Look in. Keep your finger on the place." It was a quarter to 5 in the morning, and Grandfather Reifer, as was his custom, had risen to recite the entire *sefer* (book) of *Tehillim* (Psalms). After this, he would study the Talmud until 7:30, then attend morning prayers, and at 9 o'clock return home for a quick breakfast.

A street in Chrzanow

Following breakfast, he would hasten to the warehouse, breaking off in the afternoon for another session of Talmud study. He was a man of punctilious habits, who followed this demanding routine unswervingly. His young grandchild was staying with him for an extended period of two months. This morning he had awakened his grandson with the words: "Shmuel, wake up — you are 4-and-a-half years old already. You are no longer an infant. You must join me every day in saying *Tehillim.*" The boy, rubbing the sleep from his eyes, dared not refuse, however inviting his white feather pillow, for his grandfather's word was law.

Soon, when his breakfast of milk and cake was over, Yakob would come to fetch him for *cheder*. Yakob was a gentile employed in the warehouse, whom grandfather had hired to accompany the small boy to and from *cheder*, for the *cheder* was situated a long way down the street and necessitated crossing the busy main road. Here, the young child would spend several hours in study, punctuated by periods of playing time. Slowly the hours turned round until suddenly there was the massive, genial figure of Yakob, framing the doorway, ready to take his hand. All the way along the darkening streets Yakob would softly relate stories of his childhood in the Carpathian mountains, wondrous tales of gypsies, peasants and mountain folk. The boy could almost hear the gentle bleating of goats, the shriller sound of mountain pipes, but then he would look up, and above him the lighted windows of Grandfather's apartment building loomed. They had arrived.

Grandfather Reifer was a man of quite prodigious energy. Apart from his numerous business interests, he was a devout *chassid*, and would visit his *Rebbe* three or four times a year. He owned two adjoining buildings. The one on the right housed his own *Beis HaMidrash*, and on the left, his office adjacent to the timberyard. Many would visit the apartment with the express purpose of seeking grandfather's counsel, for he was widely recognized as a G-d fearing and wise member of the community. Grandmother Reifer, by contrast, was sickly and delicate. She was diagnosed as a diabetic while several of her eight children were still young and, being ailing, it was left to her energetic husband to organize the household, as well as his multitudinous other affairs.

"Shmuel, Shmuel," she was calling from the sofa. "Are you home?" and as he was led shyly into the grandly furnished room, still clasping Yakob's hand in his own, he was greeted by, "And what did you learn at *cheder*, my child?"

"Grandmother, Grandmother," he cried out, feeling the touch of her parchment-thin skin under his fingers, but she was gone. He had been dreaming. It was all gone, and welling up inside him he felt a sense of loss as deep and irrevocable as death itself. In point of fact, he was two stories above the very room he had entered in his dream, but, he reflected, it was as good as gone. Three stories below lay the pavements of the street he had once trod so innocently with Yakob. And he knew, in a sudden flash of intuition, that this too was gone. That sweet, trusting innocence of childhood had utterly flown, like the darkness at the touch of daylight.

Grandmother — Rochel Feigel Reifer

A Childhood Incident

They were in a forest in the mountains. The trees reached up and formed a thick, intertwining pattern, blocking out even the hot sun. They were in a small country place, perhaps an hour's train ride from Chrzanow. It was situated not too far from where his great-grandfather had once owned a farm. With a few friends, they had set out in good spirits to spend the day in carefree fashion, roaming the forest, climbing trees, darting from boulder to boulder in the ice-cold mountain streams that criss-crossed the forests, picnicking on the sandwiches of cold meat that his mother had packed for them. An unexpected swishing of the trees caught the boys' attention, next a flurry of sweeping, black robes and white surplices. Novices from the neighboring monastery were bearing down on them in purposeful fashion. The first neared Shmuel's friend, Hirschel, a pale, serious-looking boy of 10. The novice reached over and delivered a stinging blow across his cheek. "*Zhid,* Jewboy!" Hirschel blinked back the tears, tasting blood in his mouth. "Why? Why?" his bewildered expression seemed to ask. "Why?" The age-old question ... it flew past the forest branches to the birds, arching their way across the intensely blue summer sky.

"Why?" The birds caught the question and carried it with them heavenward. None of the boys escaped the novices' attentions that day. Each one bore the marks of their encounter, one in a purple welt delivered by a well-aimed boot across the thigh, another in a swelling, rising visibly on the forehead.

Shaken to the core, they painfully made their way to the local police station. They looked a pitiful enough sight, this tearful group of young boys.

"And what have we here?" asked the village officer. He was a heavy, coarse-looking man who looked up from his desk, a semi-amused glint in his eye.

They told their story, expanding on all the sorry details. The sergeant's amusement grew. He called over his shoulder to his colleague.

"Here are a few young Jew-boys come to complain about being given a hiding by our friends on the hill! What do you think we should do about it, eh, eh?"

At this, they both burst out in a hearty, almost good-natured sounding laugh, as if the boys, too, ought to share their joke.

"Go home, and get your mothers to dry your eyes," they rejoined.

The boys turned to leave, the hearty laughter resounding in their ears. Again, the sense of bewilderment. Was the world topsy-turvy? Were they missing some vital link here, some information to which everyone else but they was privy?

That evening this link was finally supplied by Shmuel's father, as he painstakingly cleaned the dirt from his son's cuts: "Don't you know my child, you are a Jew?" and he emphasized the last word softly, as if that word alone held the key to the entire mystery. And then he added: "Always remember, if a Jew gets one kick, he should be happy he did not receive two!"

But the sense of bewilderment, of injustice, had never truly left him. It was here still, it lay down with him in this narrow space as he dozed, and arose with him as he lifted his head. It swelled in his breast, as he heard the imperious, megaphoned shouting, "Raus, raus," and watched the trembling crowd spill onto the streets, in twos and threes, in slow uncoordinated response.

Why, why, the same question, which his friend Hirschel had asked on that sun-dappled day, and to which he had never truly found a satisfactory answer. And it seemed to him that the sneering laughter which still rang in his ears had somehow found its way into the thinly-veiled German contempt, contempt which now stalked the Polish streets as their jackboots tore into a frightened child or an old man, contempt as they hacked off a *chassid*'s beard and *peyos*, exposing flesh and bone beneath the smooth cheek. The mystery, he knew, was somehow contained in the 'laughter,' and the German laughter as they did their work was essentially the same laugh as the police officer had exulted in after that day in the forest. It was a twisted laugh, closer to a sneer, indeed, a cosmic laugh. But signifying what? The self-satisfied laughter of the audience who sees the clown fall flat on his face into a pot of paint? Sometimes Shmuel thought that the arrogant taunting German laughter actually contained an element of fear in it, fear of something totally unknown and incomprehensible.

Chrzanow the Shtetl

Dawn was beginning to streak across the sky. Again, the sun would rise on Chrzanow, but for how many days would the sun rise, the boy wondered, on Jewish Chrzanow? For this he knew with some kind of sixth sense — that what had been occurring for weeks and months since the day the Germans had boldly walked into his hometown, had something of an apocalyptic nature in its character. And one thought hammered dully in his brain, like rain on an autumn day, more perhaps than the perilous nature of his present position — would things ever return to being as they were before? What fate held for those dragged from their narrow overcrowded sleeping quarters in those dense, violent nights, was only whispered on street corners in hasty exchanges, but never mentioned by name, for who can name the unnameable? In 1939, what is now commonplace knowledge was as unthinkable as the sky falling in on the earth, or the sun ceasing to rotate around our planet. But beneath the optimistic predictions — "We are useful, we serve as hard labor"; "They will work us hard, true, but they can never afford to dispense with us. Meanwhile, we must bide our time " — was a bone-deep knowledge of the strange nature of the barbed-wire enclosures being built deep in the Polish forests. This then was the ambiguous state of mind which pervaded the downtrodden ghetto dwellers. What the boy tried to hold onto in his mind, as though he knew its teetering precariousness, was the status of the Chrzanow of his childhood, Chrzanow, in all its whole dear precious ordinariness.

Chrzanow could well have represented any of a thousand Polish *kehillos* dotted across the length and breadth of this sprawling country. It was home to such Torah luminaries as the *Keser Torah* and the *Beis Yechezkel*. Actually, there was scarcely a Polish *kehillah* that could not boast at least one or two names of equal stature. Of its claim that its incumbent first rabbi was instated no less than two centuries previously, this was nothing remarkable. Nor is the fact that of thirty-five thousand inhabitants, over twelve thousand were Jews, and that of these most were staunchly religious. That on the Shabbos day an atmosphere of other worldliness reigned, for most shops were Jewish owned and as such were closed on this day of rest — again, this could scarcely lay claim for attention. Children wove deftly in and out of the groups of caftaned, fur-hatted men, strolling at a leisurely pace homeward from synagogue. The children were mostly earlocked, wearing the pillboxed hats customary of the *chassidic* sects of the time. At home, the women waited, ears straining for footsteps on the shabby linoleum hallways of apartment buildings. Then the distinct rap on the door, which would signal their husband's homecoming. Heavenly fragrances awaited the menfolk as they stepped over their doorways — spicy whiffs of heavy *cholent*, redolent of home comforts, repose, time-honored traditions, the mysterious mixture of materialism and spirituality which has always been the hallmark of Judaism.

Nor was the story which had circulated and been told wryly in Chrzanow environs at all unique. It so happened that the petrol station situated on the road running between Katowice and Cracow was owned by an Orthodox Jew by the name of Schiff. It was therefore closed on Shabbos. Now, those poor unfortunates who ran out of petrol on Friday afternoon would have to wait until three stars reappeared in the Chrzanow sky the following night. Of all these things, we could cite a thousand, or perhaps ten thousand towns to match.

But to the boy, of course, this was unimportant. To him, it was security, the scent of childhood, the kerchiefed, devoted figure of his mother bending low over the stove. It was hurrying to *cheder* in the predawn streets, and it was warm milk and biscuits. It was the sight of Reb Berish's stooped figure, that most beloved of men, placing his marker on the Gemara, his pale features lighting up in a rare smile of extraordinary sweetness. It was Yakob's hand in his own, imitating the sound of the tinkling of gypsy bells across the Carpathian mountains, and Yakob drying the child's tears on his fraying, brownish sleeve after some childish scuffle in *cheder*. It was playing hide-and-seek in Grandfather's lumberyard among the stacks of inert, trimmed logs, or watching the horse-drawn sleigh in winter unload its shipment, to be reloaded onto the waiting trains. It was the neighing of the horses as they shifted impatiently from foot to foot, snorting great circles into the freezing air; it was stealing away to skate on the deeply frozen pond, cheeks reddening like ripe summer apples from the furious activity, clapping hands to keep warm, tearing off the gloves and then blowing on the stiffening fingers.

It was father, dressing himself in his fur-trimmed great coat to go to work in the lumberyard, or perhaps to catch a train leaving town, tapping his pocket to make sure the ticket was there. It was finally being allowed to accompany him to see the *Rebbe*, a day's journey away, the mounting excitement as the Polish countryside rolled by and every chug of the wheels brought them nearer to their destination, for all the world like some pilgrimage of old. It was thrusting your face forward, among the black-caftaned men, to catch a glimpse of the *Rebbe's* richly embroidered sleeve, the edge of his beard, the corner of his smile, so that this would then be enough foundation to tell a fellow schoolmate at *cheder*: "I saw the *Rebbe*. He nodded or winked in my direction. I caught a few crumbs from his plate."

It was all this and so much more — the sawmill awaiting him, like the beckoning finger of destiny and a way of life so ancient, so well-embedded, that it must continue to run on its precharted tracks, for there was literally nowhere else for it to go. It was the past and the future, but not this present which would surely pass, like darkening rain clouds before a storm. Somewhere, sometime, the traditional homecoming still awaited him — father, mother, brothers, sisters — of this he was certain, even though it flew in the face of all the facts as they now stood. (Sixty years later he still waits for no less than this final homecoming to be reenacted.)

The Day the Germans Came to Chrzanow

"There are so many strands to your story. Your childhood is fascinating. But tell me when the war really began for you."

"It built up gradually, of course. You could argue that it really started the day Hitler was elected chancellor. We immediately felt the tension beginning to rise in Poland. Things became hotter and hotter for us. Anti-Semitism suddenly became, as it were, legalized. What had been just a feeling lying below the surface became talked about openly. The Polish had always been great anti-Semites. Now you could palpably feel their hostility. In those years, they would say, 'Don't worry, Hitler will come soon and teach you a lesson.' Then again, you could argue that it began with the poor half-crazed Greenspan entering the German Embassy in Paris and shooting Von Rath on the thick-piled carpet. Or Kristallnacht, the 'Night of Broken Glass,' which followed. Or the passing of the Nuremberg laws."

"Why was there no public outcry."

"The world kept silent. There was an outcry by the Jews, but the Jews had no voice as such, except perhaps, American Jews."

"When did the war begin for you in Chrzanow?"

"The day the Germans just walked into Poland as easily as a child knocking down a house of cards."

And when had the 'war' begun for him, the beginning of the madness? For he tended to think of it as an infectious disease, which would rise to delirious fever pitch and then gradually abate, leaving the patient weak and chastened, but alive and ready to begin the slow convalescence process back to his former state of health. In fact, this is the way that most of the adults spoke of it. However alarming the latest reports, however miserable their condition, the old eternal Jewish optimism would continue to rise to the fore: "Things will improve." "This is the worst. After this, things can only start to get better."

Monday. It had been a Monday, the boy lying in the narrow hideout remembered. On that day, if any of Chrzanow's twelve thousand-strong Jewish community still entertained any fanciful notions that this was to be simply 'another war' for them, these conceptions were quickly shattered with one metaphoric thud of the enemy's boot. All Jews were ordered immediately to assemble in their synagogue while their houses were searched. This was done under the pretext of searching for ammunition. In fact, the Germans took anything they could gainfully lay their hands on — jewelry, gold and silver, even food. How many Germans there were, it was impossible to assess, but they seemed to be swarming everywhere, to have occupied Chrzanow's every nook and cranny with alarming efficiency. The streets were replete with evidence of the new military command, as heavily armed German soldiers roamed here and there, their sole purpose being to strike terror in the hearts of the populace. Each day brought new reports of the tightening noose until, within weeks, they hardly knew how they had been converted from free men into trembling ghetto dwellers.

The first onslaught was focused on that badge of the traditional or chassidic Jew, the beard. It would seem that this represented a grave affront to the German notion of hygiene and respectability. Accordingly, whenever a beared Jew was sighted, he was savagely attacked. Whatever the Germans had on hand — bayonets, razors, hacksaws — were used to hack off the offending beard, and it mattered not if while removing the beard handfuls of skin and flesh would come away with it. When no instruments were available, the soldier's hand itself would suffice to do the job, and incredible as it may seem, beards were frequently set on fire. The crude barbarism of the soldiers of the Third Reich seemed to know no bounds. It was as if a kind of raging furor had been unleashed onto the streets, a flowing molten, boiling river, the source of which was uncertain and unclear. It was as if this anger, this contempt, this murderous intent, this bloodlust, would grow and grow apace — while it was being given vent to — rather than, according to natural laws, abate. If the sight of a stricken Jew, his face streaming with blood, would not appease this supra-normal anger,what would?

Yom Kippur 1939

The boy was remembering, reliving all the scenes which, in reality, he scarcely needed to relive for they swam before his eyes every waking moment. It was Yom Kippur, the holiest day of the Jewish calendar. He was standing next to his father in a white shrouded synagogue. This year the prayers were more anguished: "Forgive us for we have sinned." For what was being visited upon them now must be the result of some backsliding, some evil-doing, noted by their Father in Heaven. It was He alone who could reverse the terrifying turn of events, and effect a true deliverance. Consequently, the tears flowed more copiously on this Yom Kippur than on others. The boy shuddered, trembled visibly as the next event seemed to transpire before his eyes. The reader had just reached the most moving part of the service, the *U'nesaneh Tokef* prayer, "It is true that You alone are the One Who judges, proves, and bears witness ... All mankind will pass before you like members of the flock ... On Rosh Hashanah they will be inscribed and on Yom Kippur they will be sealed ... How many will pass from the earth and how many will be created, who will live and who will die, who will die at his predestined time and who before his time, who by water, who by fire, who by sword, who by beast —," when a sound at once of breaking glass and of the heavy doors being forced, stopped him in mid-sentence, mid-breath almost. Silence. A silence as deep as the grave reigned for perhaps thirty seconds. Then, the noises, the terrible violent, arrogant shouting, the curses, the imprecations, to which, if it was feasible, they had grown accustomed these past few weeks. And the shouting! It was possible to distinguish a few sounds, *"Verfluchte Jüden, raus, raus ..."* The boy had slipped his hand into his father's, involuntarily, when it had begun. Now, as he withdrew it, he realized it was dripping with perspiration. Next, a high-ranking officer stepped forward. In a quieter, deceptively more controlled voice, he asked: "Who are your leaders? We will not harm the rest of you, but we want ten of your leaders to come forward."

The boy's eyes were drawn to that of the German officer. They were the coldest, most piercing, inhuman blue he had ever seen. In fact, they belonged to a man who had already become somewhat notorious as a Jew-hunter, *Obersturmführer* Major Linde — but this the boy did not yet know. Linde's credentials in the Jew-hunting business were quite impressive. He had swiftly settled matters in Biala-Podolski's prisoner-of-war camp just a few weeks earlier. He had segregated the Jewish prisoners of war from the Poles, and summarily dispatched them with single pistol shots aimed to the head. One of them had been young Perlstein from Chrzanow. He, a soldier, had originally been arrested for the crime of accumulating 'food' in the house. This was an offense punishable by instant death. Now, as *Obersturmführer* Linde repeated his request in the seemingly reasonable terms of a businessman dictating letters to his secretaries, a sort of a shudder ran through the gathered crowd. In their white *kittels,* and shod in compliance with the law of this holiest of days, they seemed to have visibly shrunk and paled in the last few moments.

Major Linde waited. He knew the value of letting his victims 'sweat,' anticipating his next move.

"Very well," he continued, still in the affable, reasonable tone he had been employing until that moment. "Where is your Eltersrat? Are there any of its members praying in this synagogue?"

Ashen faced, two members stepped forward, bowing a little, as if with a reflex movement.

"I will give you five minutes. I will provide you with pen and paper. You in turn will write down ten names, ten people who carry the most weight in this town. Your five minutes begin now," he said with a glance at his watch.

The two men hesitated, glanced at each other, then began to scribble furiously, in contravention of Jewish law, their papers resting on the reader's lectern.

"Your five minutes are up," the now shrill voice interrupted them. "Would ... please step forward," the voice continued, reading off the list in staccato fashion.

The boy watched horrified as his grandfather's imposing figure began to stir in its place, several rows ahead of them. His had been the last name, but on the list. He began to move purposefully to the front of the synagogue, until he had joined the line of men now lined up and facing *Obersturmführer* Linde, who now permitted a wry smile of satisfaction to cross his ascetic features.

⸾⸾

"You mention the name Obersturmführer Linde many times. Why does he stand out in your memory?"

"You know, this Linde, he hated Jews with a bottomless fury. When he saw a Jew, he would fly into a terrible rage. It was as if he became quite literally a beast who wished to tear this poor Jew limb from limb. I had the feeling, perhaps I am wrong, that he was essentially a 'cultivated man.' Only a German could be capable of this — this transformation into a chayah ra'ah, a wild devouring beast, barely human. This is the one aspect of it all which I will never truly fathom."

Obersturmführer Linde

The boy wondered and wondered about *Obersturmführer* Linde. In the coming months and years of terror he was to have the opportunity to study at firsthand many men of his ilk. Some of the SS and their assistants were, in the pure sense of the words, hoodlums, mindless criminals, possessed with and permitted to give vent to an endless appetite for torture and murder. These, he would always find easier to understand. What motivated them was the promise of an extra bottle or two of liquor, or cigarettes. Yes, it was these trivial incentives with which those roving purveyors of murder, the *Einsatztruppen* reputedly positioned themselves behind their machine guns to carry out the "great work in the East." But men like these? Linde seemed to be a professional man, and the boy warranted that in civilian life he had been an upper echelon office worker, perhaps even a lawyer or an accountant. Perhaps, one day sitting in his office, doing his customary overtime, he had had a sudden feeling that his life would continue like this forever — the yearly small increases in salary, the enforced thriftness, with a wife and two children to support. Then, as the decades rolled by, the turning into a carbon copy of his superior — a bent, bespectacled trivial-minded fellow. So that when a friend in the office asked him to attend a party meeting, he went just to see what it was like, and emerged shaken by the sheer breadth of vision a new Germany presented.

The propaganda about the Jews had not touched him closely, for he had been on convivial terms with one or two of his Jewish neighbors. He would often stop for a chat with old Marius who had served in the First World War with distinction, and sported a row of medals to prove it. They seemed decent enough people, even if wearing a certain anxious look in the eye. Later he would come to consider again this anxious look, this inability to look you directly in the eye, like a good German, as a means of disguising a centuries-old burden of guilt. At heart, he would continue to believe that much of the anti-Jewish propaganda was excessive, but here, at last, was an opening out of vistas, not just for the fatherland, but for his own life, grown staid with respectable monotony. Here was a picture painted in the boldest terms of a glorious new future and it was as if the sun had come out on a rainy day and touched his world and washed it in its golden hues. And it was as if he, too, was being washed by this noon glow, and as if he could finally see a future for himself, unhemmed by pettiness and trivialities, soaring on the wings of this shining florescence.

His progress through the party was swift, for his professional skills were useful. When war ultimately broke out, dispatched to Poland in its earliest days as a now high-ranking officer, he had come up against the 'Jewish thing' again. However, having been exposed at firsthand to that lowest and most debased of creatures, the *Ostjude*, he was becoming more and more deeply convinced that the Fuhrer possessed a deeper insight into these matters than he had at first grasped. As they marched into Polish border towns, Jews stood in groups, the women heavily kerchiefed, surrounded by six or seven 'brats', the men, bearded and caftaned, and always the eyes furtive, anxious, shifty. They looked greasy, and, making a mental connection under the influence of party propaganda, diseased, or at any rate not commensurate with the concepts of the new German superbreed. *Untermenschen.* He began to see the world in broader terms. Individual life was no longer of ultimate importance. No, it was only the 'goal,' the 'great goal,' clear, wholesome and shining, towards which they all were striding, confident and unafraid, which mattered now. Words echoed at party meetings hammered dully through his brain: "The Jews are our misfortune. The Jews are the misfortune of the world."

When summoned to Biala-Podolski 'to see to things' there, his first position of real responsibility, it had been simple enough to 'prove' himself. They died easily enough; the old adage, "like sheep to the slaughter," rose to the forefront of his mind. Why did they not strike out, even in futile rebellion? He noticed then a phenomenon which would give vent in him to an even colder, more implacable anger — they simply followed his orders. He quietly ordered them to line up. This they did and then each in turn stepped forward to be shot. It was as if the fear had immobilized them so that their very thinking capacities ceased to function. After he had shot one or two, their brains pulverized to a pulp as they hit the ground, to continue to shoot was easy. No, not easy, he might better describe it as necessary. And from that moment the 'fury' never left him.[1]

Grandfather and the others were marched away. Those left behind watched their grimly retreating backs. As they left and the great doors closed easily behind them, a low buzz erupted. What should they do now? Finally, the Rabbi, an aging figure who seemed, if it was possible, to have grown whiter in the last few moments, banged on the lectern:

"We must not allow them to succeed," he said in a trembling voice. "If we permit them to halt our prayers on this Holiest of Days, then know that they have won." His voice rose to a crescendo, "And G-d forbid," he added in a low voice. "No," he continued, "we must entreat our merciful Father in Heaven for *rachamim* (mercy) for those whom we have just seen taken hostage, and for all our suffering fellow Jews in these dark days." At this his voice finally broke into the sob which had lain beneath the surface of his words all along.

So, prayers resumed. This was the way Yom Kippur was spent in Chrzanow in 1939.

Horrifying Days at Gestapo Headquarters

Grandfather Reifer, in marching with firm step out of the synagogue on the Day of Atonement, effectively disappeared for the next few days. All efforts by his frantic family to trace his whereabouts proved to no avail. He may as well have dropped off the face of the planet. It was only on *erev* Sukkos, when a sharp knock resounded at the Reifer's front door, and the specter of Grandfather

---

1. Linde took his own life in a Hamburg prison, the night before he was due to be extradited to Poland.

Reifer's crumpled frame being carried, or half-dragged by two equally defeated men, turned up on the dark threshold, that they were able to piece together his story. The 75-year-old had been held for most of his term of imprisonment in a dungeon cell. The stone walls reeked with damp and greenish mildew. The only light issued from a small barred window. At first, the setting — punctuated as it was by cries of real human agony which seemed to issue from nowhere and stop as inexplicably as they had begun — seemed to him surreal, as if he had somehow been cast back in time to some medieval epoch of torture and beastliness. Alone in his cell, he prayed for whatever was to befall him either to begin or to end. He saw no one, spoke to no one. A little bread and water were poked through the barred doors twice a day.

When summoned at last, he found in himself an ability to retreat from this strange and troubling present, back to the days on ... St., the tables ornately set for festive meals, the house ringing with laughter and conviviality. The Gestapo faces, cold and calculating, retreated, and even the torturous blows, when they began to draw blood, could not find him. This enraged them, seeing that they could not reach the core of the man. The blows, the imprecations rained thicker and thicker, until at last they became a sea of human pain, each new blow indistinguishable from the one before. At last, the heavy stick broke on his back, and he was half dragged back to his subterranean lair. He must have lain on the stone floor, his blood seeping into the stone, for a day or two. Once he remembered leaning on one elbow and tearing some scrap off his shirt and trying to bind his wounds, for he knew that slowly the steady drip, drip of blood, of his life's force, would lead him into the final darkness that is death. He had not known, he remembered thinking, the answers to their questions, had never known them. Perhaps, he had not been intended to. Certainly, it seemed to him that the issue was beyond questions or answers, and had already been decided elsewhere, for him and the others. The very next thing to wash over his consciousness was an entirely unfamiliar scraping and creaking of metal. It seemed to him that the door was opening.

"Are you Reifer?"

"On your feet."

As inexplicably as he had been gathered into this place of no answers, he was spewed out of it. Thrust onto the floor of a police van, he found himself at the corner of his son's street, whose address he had given. Here he lay, looking up from the comfort of the pavement at the familiar line of balconies, and trailing plants, and washing lines, virtually incapable of rising to his feet. As night fell, two pairs of strange hands gathered him up roughly and deposited him, rather like a parcel, at his son's door.

Elsewhere in Chrzanow and eventually in the rest of Poland, this was a pattern that was to be repeated. In every town hostages, deemed to be men of some importance, were seized. Usually a group of ten was preferred. Of those taken from the synagogue that day, one was the town's locksmith. He was not taken as was Grandfather Reifer to the Gestapo headquarters, which was the real name for that region of darkness where he had been incarcerated for those days and nights, but to a trench some way outside the town. Here, in company with other Jews gathered at that place, he was ordered to bury dead horses. It was a symbolic action intended to convey to them more than a notion, that the time was not far off when their own human remains would be treated with less respect than this. As they shoveled earth, it seemed to them, and not without reason, that it was themselves that they were burying beneath the unyielding Polish soil — themselves and their simple, seemingly inalienable human right to be brought to *kever Yisroel*. Along with this, too, they were totally burying the notion of what one human being owes another in terms of respect and decency, so that it was perfectly in tune with these unmentionable sentiments that ran like an electric current beneath the heavy thud of their spades, striking earth — that as they shoveled they were subject, too, to a steady stream of abuse. Lashed, spat upon, propaganda statements rose to the surface, almost of their own accord, like a filthy froth on a dirt-encrusted glass — statements that were now being screamed out around the parameters of the New Europe: *"The Jews are the misfortune of the world. The Jews started the war!"*

And when the Jews lapsed, as they would at this provocation, into their age-old mainstay — prayer, the final, definitive statement: "What is that you are mumbling, you filthy Jew? Where is your G-d? Why doesn't He come and help you now? Hah, hah!"

And it seemed then, in those moments, to the Jews, religious and non-religious alike, that the essence of this strangest, bitterest of all wars, was encapsulated in that question. It was the 'G-d-like' image that the Germans wished to kill in the Jew, or no less than the Jewish G-d. Yet, at the same time, they labeled these same Jews 'scum of the earth, vermin.' The paradox was that hatred of that dimension could only be reserved for, and provoked by, something worthy of that hatred. These were the beginnings of that struggle, primeval and all-embracing — the all or nothing, which spawned the inexplicable 'thing' which was to come. It was something still measureable now in these days of single acts of terror lapsing into occasional or sporadic murders. It was like the moments before a threatening tornado when the wind, which begins as something containable, gathers momentum and, breaking a certain barrier of velocity, is suddenly recognizable as being out of the ordinary in scale, potentially deadly, potentially catastrophic. In this spirit of 'measuring the wind,' the days and weeks after occupation in Poland passed.

"Was there nothing that could have been done to avert what was to come? You had warnings."

"Oh, yes. We had some idea, but then we always hoped with a Jewish optimism. 'A Yid git zich an eitzah! (A Jew finds a solution!)' is the Yiddish expression and this epithet kept our spirits up. A Jew always survives. This much has *been promised. But of what they really had planned for us, we had no inkling. Who could have?! You see, it simply had no precedent and men are strangely unimaginative creatures. What has never happened will, by definition, never happen."*

The Ghetto

The boy in the attic remembered certain things above others from the last few weeks and months. In truth, he was hardly a boy, and he was now trembling on the brink of adulthood. But it seemed to him that what had happened to him — more than anything else — was that his childhood had been stripped away from him, relentlessly peeled away, leaving him denuded and defenseless. It was not only the innocence of the past which he had lost, but that assurance of the future, which is what a secure childhood brings, that things would go well with him in the way in which his

Grandfather's House

Jews being rounded up in the Ghetto

parents had planned and envisioned on many a quiet night, lying
awake, as words of deliberation passed between them — that he
would take over the sawmill, marry, become a respected Chrzanow
householder, and a staunch *chassid*. All this he saw slipping relentlessly away from him, as the madness escalated. And how long
could this homey vision be maintained against the fury? If, as the
grownups argued, it was a storm which would rise to a murderous
crescendo, and would then abate having spent itself, there would
then be a chance of returning, like survivors of a great catastrophe,
to pick up the pieces, in the same old places, to rebuild and con-
solidate, to carry on in the same pattern so seamlessly that, eventually, after a few years, no one would be able to guess that there
had ever been a threat of this proportion to the structure. This,
then, was the eternal Jewish optimism, which lifted them through
each day of new despair. In truth, this was something so different
in dimension from anything known before in the long, often frightful history of the Jews, that, looking back, it was almost impossible
to foretell, and simply move cleanly out of the way.

What he remembered from all those weeks and months was first the noises, the megaphoned nasal sneering shouts commanding them to go from one place to another like cattle. "Vacate your homes, hand over your food, your valuables!" It seemed that the demands grew more and more outrageous, beginning with objects, but objects which had formed their past. The silver candlesticks, a family heirloom which had been passed down lovingly from generation to generation, and which the Polish Catholic maid polished every Friday till you could see your own distorted image in them —- these were the first things to be bartered in the Reifer household. How could Shabbos be ushered in without them? His mother's engagement and wedding rings, spice boxes, *Kiddush* cups all followed suit. These things were in reality not 'dead' things at all, but possessed a 'quickness' and 'aliveness' that tore at their owners' hearts as they handed them over, until it seemed to the boy that they were actually engaged in bartering for their lives. The ornate spice box was given in exchange for the right to subsist on their meager rations.

After a while, it became apparent to him that what they were receiving was not a fair exchange. When they gave in to one demand, another, more outrageous than the first, followed hard on its heels. He knew that the grownups knew this too. He could see it in the peculiar despondency of the glances that were exchanged furtively between them when they thought that no eyes were upon them. Thus, when the orders came to change location, to simply get up and leave the brick and mortar of their pasts, it was not so difficult to accomplish this. Had they not already surrendered most of what made Jagielonska Street into something peculiarly individual, endowed with the special appellation of home? It was relatively easy, then, to load up most of their remaining belongings, the meager clothing, the few books and photographs left to them, the blankets, pots and pans, and join the 'poor' sea of humanity with their pasts similarly loaded onto a wheelbarrow. And somehow, at that moment, the Jewish past resurrected itself, the *golus Yid*, the *luftmensch*, never putting down real roots — at home wherever the wind blew him. This was the true face of the Jew. What they had been living out in between the intermittent pogroms and Jew hunts in their relatively peaceful coexistence, was nothing more substantial than a dream.

The final act had come in the construction of high ghetto walls, which was carried out under penalty of death by the Jews themselves. Something in the Jewish makeup 'needed' segregation from their gentile neighbors. Even the most assimilated Jew accepted this genetic difference in his heart of hearts. That is why the secular Jew fought so vehemently against this very concept. It was as if the Germans were saying, "The Jews will be happier in their ghettos. They create their ghettos anyway as they go along." And then, of course, there were the lies about infection, the age-old lies, bolstered by centuries of propaganda and distortion. The high walls were needed to protect the population from the Jews who were, as everyone clearly recognized, disease-ridden vermin. After all, had not the Aryan the inherent right to breathe unpolluted, Jew-free air?

The Reifers themselves were crowded into a small flat, with three other families. There was scarcely room to turn around, to stretch out, certainly no room for that most scarce of luxuries, to think, to be alone, to meditate. Everywhere one fell over another, another who also wore or mirrored the same expression to be found on your face, the typical ghetto dweller's perpetually anxious look. 'Have I room to sleep, to wash, to eat, to breathe? What will the next day bring, what new laws or indignities? How much less space can the

Mother — Rivkah Jeret Reifer

human frame occupy?' They felt that they were being squeezed and squeezed remorselessly. Every able-bodied man was required to work and would be sent out from the ghetto in the labor squads, at first light, and return late at night. The boy was enlisted in one of these squads. The remuneration was minimal, one hundred marks a month of which fifty marks had to be immediately returned to the SS. Rations were less than meager — half a kilogram of bread a week, one egg, some potatoes, radishes, kohlrabi. Meat was not to be had. Immediately, a black market was set up so that certain items could be bartered. However, this was an extremely risky business for, if caught, the punishment was immediate death. However, survival was only made possible by the acquisition of some extras.

Every ghetto dweller was required to carry his identity card at all times. Failure to produce this at demand would invoke instant retribution. Death was the specter of the ghetto. It stalked the mean ghetto streets, no longer an outrageous sight, but something expected, of an everyday nature. Occasional shots and cries would ring out within the ghetto environs intermittently, or death would visit in more gradual ways, on the heels of slow starvation, the rampant ghetto diseases, or simply the ghetto despair. What soon became apparent, after several weeks and months of this existence, was that death was somehow at the end of it all. It was indeed, and this dawning came more slowly — it was nothing less than the supreme purpose of these strange anachronistic enclosures.

An Interlude

The boy was remembering something else, outside the ghetto, an interlude. There had been peril in it, but there was no escaping the danger in those days. Everything was, simply put, 'dangerous.' To walk in the middle of the sidewalk or on the cobbled streets themselves, to look an SS officer straight in the face, or to evade his eye, to look too furtive or too relaxed, to hurry overmuch or linger overmuch — nothing, literally no moment of the day, escaped these kinds of impossible choices. The gray matter of the brain seemed to be permanently harried trying to unravel these recurring riddles. But the riddle which lay coiled like a snake at the bottom of it all was life or death, no less.

By dint of a combination of daring and desperation, Shmuel Reifer, his father and uncle managed that first summer in the ghetto, to escape to Grandfather Reifer's farm, deep in the Polish countryside. The ghetto was an open one, which meant that traffic was permitted in and out of its walls. However, the three could not risk riding on a train or bus, which would spell instant discovery. Instead, covering their yellow 'Jude' star with their worn jackets, they decided to walk to their destination through the Polish summer night. They walked steadily, saying little to one another, mindful of their ultimate purpose. Within the ghetto walls, behind the ugly brick partitions and watchtowers, the other family members were literally starving, and this was the course of action they had finally decided on through long nights of discussion.

"Shmuel, keep up my boy!" his father urged, rubbing his hands, panting a little.

Uncle Reifer began to softly hum a popular tune.

"Walking, the finest exercise in the world, eh boy," as if they were for all the world engaged on a pleasurable summer hike. "Stretch the limbs, eh, after being bent over your Gemara all day long," neglecting to mention the unpalatable fact that, on the contrary, the boy had been torn from his studies some bitter months since, and had been enlisted in the backbreaking squads, shoveling snow or earth outside Chrzanow's parameters.

This is how, if the boy recalled correctly, they talked in those days, skirting the real issues, pretending things were just as they had always been. There was no choice in this, this was simply how they felt compelled to talk, more to themselves than to others, in order to survive.

Dawn was just beginning to streak across the sky, first blackness giving way to gray, then the palest of pink florescences.

Ahead of them stretched fields and meadows, still peaceful in the dawn, still untouched by the manifold wakings of men. Here lived Polish countryfolk, bigoted to be sure, and deeply anti-Semitic. On the other hand, the German presence was much less marked here than in the towns. Here they could find work, and perhaps smuggle small amounts of food to those incarcerated within the ghetto walls. And this was the way it happened. Laboring as farmhands for some toughened Polish farmer, they managed to smuggle a little butter, a little milk, back to Chrzanow's ghetto, with Shmuel Reifer's younger brother, who rode out to meet them each day on his makeshift bicycle. In this abnormal way they passed that dying summer, sometimes pausing from their work for a moment to savor the sun's caress on their too thin faces, until winter forced them once again, unwillingly, back to the familiar ghetto walls.

Back in the Ghetto

"How did you live in the ghetto? What happened to the quality of your life?"

"Quality of life? What life? We were being 'squeezed' towards the brink like a lemon which is being slowly and systematically emptied of its zest. This was the enemy's plan. They knew the spirit of the Jew, and like all our enemies of old, it was our spirit they wanted, even more than our bodies. Otherwise, they knew that with what they labeled as our 'habitual cunning,' we would in the end outwit them. This was why, later, we were to see their fanatical zeal for numbers and lists. They were afraid to let even one of us escape — afraid with a deep and terrible fear. In fact, I somehow think that they were more afraid of us than we of them, in a metaphysical sense. But we did outwit them, in so many little ways. This is what so few people know. We strove with all our might to cling to the bulwark of the halachah (Jewish Law),

*knowing that here was guidance for all situations, even these
unthinkable ones in which we now found ourselves. Can you
believe that in the ghettos, under the shadow of death, we kept
the Yomim Tovim after a fashion?"*

〰〰

Pesach was drawing near in the ghetto. Each landmark of time,
once waited for in loving anticipation, had now assumed the bitter
rancorous taste of dead autumn leaves. Thinking, planning ahead
was difficult in their new roles as 'ghetto *menschen*,' for more than
their bodies, it was their brains which were assailed daily by new,
ever stricter lunatic contingencies. It was their brain and beyond
that their spirit which was bearing the brunt of the repeated blows
— the physical confinement, terror, uncertainty, starvation, work.
Yet, remarkably, it was the spirit which not infrequently sprang
back and retaliated, as if to say: "You want my pride, my Jewish
pride, more than anything, you Nazi thugs, more than even my
body. Well, this Jewish pride will outlive you. It has outlived others whose empires now lie prone and crumpled in the dust. You
force us to wear the yellow star 'Jude'; well, we can do so with
pride, *mit stoltz*, and not with shame.

To live a life guided as ever by the parameters of *halachah*, ignor-
ing the minutiae of Nazi terror, represented, under these impossible
circumstances, a tremendous triumph. So that if one April morning
Shmuel Reifer's father turned to his family and whispered:
"Matzos, how are we going to get hold of matzos for Pesach?" —
this was no less than a quiet revolution. The gentile 'Sapieha' — a
titled nobleman who owned some of the villages surrounding
Chrzanow — with whom the boy's father had had a long-standing
business connection, was accustomed to smuggle into the ghetto
the odd sackful of grain. He had been enormously fond of the family and could not bear now to think of them slowly starving to death
behind the ugly brick walls. This sack of 'Sapieha' grain now came
in exceedingly useful. It was laboriously ground by hand, but in the

utmost secrecy, for such activities were certainly punishable by death. Several unsightly-looking matzos were formed, and then baked in the simple oven. In this way, *Seder* night of that year found the Reifer family fulfilling the *mitzvah* of eating unleavened bread. Also, for the rest of the festival, they refused their bread rations, eating only potatoes.

~~~~~

Another feature of ghetto life was the ostensible banning of all religious observance. All synagogues and other institutions were closed effective immediately. This, possibly more than all the other contingencies — the meagerness of the rations, the terrible overcrowding, the lice, disease, uncertainty — this signified that their very lifeblood, their life force was being strangled. If they allowed this to happen, they would suffocate, soundlessly, become a group of enslaved, downtrodden individuals with no cohesive center to bind them. Some found a way of meeting clandestinely in oppressive rooms, whispering the well-loved words hurriedly. The words themselves gave them hope: "There is no power on earth which lasts forever. This empire of wickedness, too, will pass as other tyrannies have passed." But despite the words, their bloodshot eyes watched the doorways furtively, ears strained for any untoward sound, any change in the spat-out Germanic syllables which resounded from dawn to dusk around the ghetto streets. These, they knew, could change in an instant to something signifying immediate approach. They had plans for such intrusions, but often they would stand frozen in mid-sentence, or even mid-word, lower lips trembling uncontrollably. During these days, if one so much as looked up at one's neighbor, one might well notice tears streaming unchecked down his unshaven sunken cheeks. In this peculiar atmosphere, one would then look away just as quickly, for one could not here afford the luxury of fellow sympathy which freedom brings.

Shmuel Reifer Still in the Attic

By Shmuel Reifer's reckoning, he had been locked into the attic hideaway for almost thirty-six hours, for the sun had risen and was prepared to set again. He feared the onset of another twelve hours of darkness, for he was beginning to feel unbearably confined and alone. He was desperately hungry and thirsty, over and above the customary ghetto hunger. He had swallowed his last morsel of food as the previous night had fallen, so that a further twenty-four hours had passed since that moment. Someone would, someone must come for him, he repeated to himself over and over again. Perhaps his parents would realize what had happened and send someone to search for him, that is, providing the unthinkable had not come to pass. For the hundredth time, perhaps, he half-rose, approached the opening on his hands and knees, and both pulled and pushed in alternate spasmodic movements. But nothing happened. It was securely fastened. He was well and truly hidden, so well that he now

Reifer family residence up to 1943

feared that these four graying, peeling walls, the sill, the window beyond the sloping ceiling would indeed be his end. On all of these, his last look would rest. He would now never outlive this cruelest of wars, nor see the return of springtime to the Chrzanow streets. He would never have to observe mournfully the now permanently pained look in his mother's delicate features, or feel the penetrating gaze of the gray intelligence of his father's all-knowing eye.

"Perhaps, it is better thus," he thought, if the rumors wildly circulating in the ghetto are true. There is no 'place of resettlement' in the East, no prettified Jew towns, and if those that were gone would never return, it would surely be better to draw his last breath here. But no, he almost hissed, between cracked lips, his youth and vigor rising unbidden to the surface: "I am young. I want to live, I want to live. Whatever comes — "

"So there you were, still imprisoned in this attic. You must have thought freedom would never come! You must have despaired!"

"One loses touch with reality in a situation like that. And also speaking of these things from the comfort of our sitting room, one realizes that one would have to invent a whole new language to describe what we went through. What is 'hunger' to you? A missed meal? 'Cold,' an unheated room? 'Fear'? And so on. We were living on a different plane. Take 'fear,' for example; it was with us day and night, even in our dreams. One passes a natural barrier then, so that at a certain point one can 'feel' no more. One's whole life is fear. If we would now in our 'safe' life, experience even one-hundredth, one-thousandth part of anything we went through then, I am sure that we could not bear it.

"I always hated closed-in places since I was a young child, and there I was, locked in alone, cold, hungry, fearful for my life. So how did I bear it? I cannot explain it. I have learned *one thing from it all, I suppose, and that is never to be dependent on any human being, man or woman. This may sound hard. Does it sound that way to you?"*

"Explain what you mean."

"You see, when the war broke out, I was so sheltered — part of a large and prominent family. And then, everything was lost to me, people, places, a way of life, my own identity. I have had to reinvent myself. There is only One of Whom one can be sure and it is the all-seeing A-mighty. But people? A human being is nothing, like an unrooted plant which can be blown this way or that in the wind. A broken vessel, a fleeting dream ..."

The story of how Shmuel Reifer came eventually, on that second night of being locked in, to be released, is an interesting one, and it also involves characters who expand the scope of his story beyond the merely personal. Of course, his story has its own intrinsic worth, for even were the selfsame story to be told and retold a thousand, nay a million, or six million times, until the very details were engraved both in our hearts and in our minds, it would still be incumbent upon us to tell it just once more. In the words of the *Hagaddah*: "Were we all wise men, men of discernment, we would still be duty bound to relate the story of the Exodus from Egypt." This being so, Shmuel Reifer's story, being that of a typical Orthodox youth of 18, from the typical Polish community of Chrzanow, is worth the sum of all the other stories which have ever been told of this dark hole of human history, or will ever be told. But it also — as personal histories often do — points a finger toward another story.

A Story Within a Story

The boy's uncle (his mother's brother) was a wealthy timber merchant from Cracow named Simon Jeret. After his father passed away

Simon Jeret

at a young age, Simon had entered his father's business and supported his mother, who was left with eight young children. He had an office in Merish, Ostro-Czechoslovakia. Here he spent his weekdays, and it was here, too, that he became well-acquainted with a dashing German entrepreneur, whose name Oskar Schindler was destined to become known to the whole world.

Schindler originated from Brinitz in the Sudetenland, then part of Czechoslovakia. After the German invasion of Poland, Oskar Schindler came to Cracow as a privileged, but human, German. He sought to establish himself in business. What would later occur would pass into the annals of history, causing Oskar Schindler's name to become synonymous with that of the 'good German,' and assuring Simon Jeret of a small niche in that same history. How crucial a role Jeret came to play in the Schindler story has never quite satisfactorily been recorded.

At a loss as to how to proceed in occupied Cracow, where he grasped at once that fortunes were to be made, Schindler contacted Simon Jeret, one of the few acquaintances he could claim in that ancient city. Jeret was a well-established businessman and would be a valuable source of contacts and information. Eventually, it was proposed to Schindler, who was looking around for a factory, that the 'Emalia Fabrik,' or enamel factory, which had hitherto been in Jewish hands, had become available. Schindler took it over. Here, he was able to employ Jews from the ghetto, thereby allowing them to stay on in the ghetto for as long as possible, avoiding the mass deportations which were beginning to take place. The Emalia Fabrik produced, besides pots and pans, important components needed for the war machinery. In this way, Schindler managed to acquaint himself with the Rüstungs Commando. Later, in 1942, when the ghetto was liquidated, and the children and old people had been sent away, those of working age were placed in the concentration camp, Plazow. Schindler's Jewish workers were placed in a camp adjoining the enamel factory. As events transpired, and Schindler became fired with the ambition to save his Jewish workers from their fate of anonymous death, Simon Jeret became indispensable to him once more. Schindler needed commodities with which to bribe the Rüstungs Commando, thereby encouraging them to turn a blind eye to his

Chaya Jeret

illegal activities. Thus, he needed a perpetual supply of furs, alcohol, diamonds and real coffee, which the Germans craved above all else. So, it transpired that every night, a casual but interested bystander might have observed Simon Jeret, accompanied by a German SS guard, being marched out of the camp, carrying a significant amount of cash. He was then able to procure the commodities which were of such value to Schindler from his contacts on the black market.

This status quo, with Jeret acting as willing go-between, and Schindler, self-appointed protector of his Jews, was brought to an abrupt halt in the summer of 1944. With the Russian army now nearing Cracow, Plazow was liquidated and its Jews dispersed to Auschwitz or Gross-Rosen. It was at this point that Schindler, in fevered desperation, began compiling his famous list. The list grew more and more expansive until it included the names of twelve hundred men, women and children. He demanded from the Rüstungs Commando that their papers be released and that they be evacuated to Brinitz, his new headquarters. He intended to move all the installations of his enamel factory there to enable him, so he said, to continue his production for the war effort.

However, his plans now began to go somewhat awry. The nine hundred men on his list were sent to Gross-Rosen instead of to

Brinitz. They were detained in Gross-Rosen for five days, where they were handed the customary striped uniforms, and registered as '*lager*-dwellers.' After five days, when the error was discovered, they were dispatched on to Brinitz. In Brinitz, a camp had been set up under SS *Sturmbanführer* Leopold. Leopold had previously been an SS Fuhrer in Maidanek, where he had acquired a murderous reputation, but in Brinlitz he was bribed and controlled by Schindler. (However, once, when Schindler was arrested for misconduct, Leopold managed to send a transport of youngsters from Brinlitz to Auschwitz.)

The three hundred women on Schindler's list had an even more troublesome passage. They were sent to Auschwitz from Plazow, due to a clerical error. When three weeks had elapsed, Uncle Jeret went crying to Schindler, for his wife Chaya Jeret was among the trapped 'Schindler's women.' Uncle Jeret's Catholic friend, Ciechanowski, held a very valuable diamond in safekeeping for him, in addition to a sizeable quantity of solid-wood parquet flooring, which was a rare commodity in those days. Through Schindler, Simon Jeret contacted Ciechanowski and liquidated these assets, which were the last of his valuables. Schindler himself then sprang into action. He went again to the Rüstungs Commando to obtain vital verification of the importance of his production to the war effort. Armed with these papers, he traveled to Gestapo headquarters in Berlin, and met the head of the Jewish Department, Mr. Maurer. Mr. Maurer agreed to send a special envoy to the Gestapo who administered Auschwitz in Katowice. Here, Schindler was directed to various officials, including Mr. Dreher, Mr. Frietag, Mr. Kronau and Mr. Vaikern. As a result of these talks, a Gestapo member was dispatched to Auschwitz with the list of Schindler's three hundred women in his pocket.

Chaya Jeret would later recall that on that fateful morning, the women, now thoroughly unrecognizable, were already undressed, ready for the gas chambers. All at once, an official, brandishing a list, arrived and began reading out names. Those whose names were called were rushed to the cattle cars, where they were kept waiting for several days, not knowing what fate awaited them.

Meanwhile, the Germans, with their standard punctiliousness, were occupied in ensuring that the numbers tallied. It was only when the wagons drew in to Brinlitz station and the women saw the benignly towering figure of Schindler ahead of them, outlined against the blue mountains, that they realized that a stupendous miracle had been done for them. This was a unique event. Never in Auschwitz's whole, frightful, beyond-words history would any other convoy of Jewish 'livestock' be released back through its gates.

Schindler's connections with Uncle Jeret were not quite finished. With Russian guns pounding only miles from Brinitz two weeks before the liberation, Schindler contacted Simon Jeret in the dead of the night. He told him that he had intercepted a telegram sent to *Lagerführer* Leopold, ordering him to take all the Jews safely sheltering in Brinitz to Theresienstadt, where they would be killed. Schindler did not allow this telegram to reach Leopold. Instead, he traveled to Leopold's military unit and managed to have a false telegram dispatched, ordering him to report at once to his military unit. In this way, he managed to get rid of Leopold at the eleventh hour. However, Schindler, still apprehensive that the remaining SS personnel stationed in Brinitz would try to deport 'his Jews,' himself brought his people rifles and ammunitions, urging them to defend themselves, should this contingency arise.

Through the remarkable agency of Schindler, both Jeret and his wife survived the war, although their three children perished. The unique collaboration between Schindler the German, and Jeret the Jew, had likewise saved the lives of hundreds of his fellow-Jews.

Notably, it was Mr. Jeret who, at the moment of liberation, presented Schindler with a golden ring. This ring had been made by fellow Brinlitz inmates from the only gold available to them,

Jeret's golden crowns, and was inscribed with the Talmudic saying: "He who saves one Jewish soul, it is as if he has saved an entire world."

To which Schindler ceremoniously replied: "Thank you, Mr. Jeret."

≈≈≈

This story within a story impinges on Shmuel Reifer's story only with the lightest of touches. However, it is worth remembering, too, that during those terrible years, there was a man such as Schindler, whose protection was afforded to those fortunate enough to fall under his care. However, men like him were pitifully few, and most Jews, like our protagonist, were exposed to the alternative — which was the pitiless, murderous fury of the Third Reich. For most there was no gentle ark of shelter from the storm, no benign rescuer outwitting the regime. On the contrary, they were entirely alone, entirely unprotected.

How Schindler's story touches on our own is quite simple in that the door to the attic hideout was eventually opened, after Shmuel Reifer's two days of loneliness and fear, by two relatives. One was the boy's aunt, Chaya Jeret, wife of the aforementioned Simon Jeret, who was trying to find a relative in Chrzanow, and the other, a distant relative, Sonia Lednitzer. Knowing of the hideout in Grandfather Reifer's house, these two young women had gone there and, noticing the door securely locked from the outside, had unbolted it out of curiosity. When, minutes later, out from the hiding place had crawled the 18-year-old Shmuel, their astonishment was unfeigned. But in these days, one did not linger too long in rumination over unlikely events, for the very fabric of their lives was beyond belief. One simply took things as they came, one's brain moving always one step ahead. Conversely, it was possible to just die, frozen in slow motion or immobility. So if she said: "Shmuel, what are you doing here?" not pausing to hear the explanation, and if he asked, "Aunt Chaya, Sonia, what brings you to

Chrzanow?" this might be closest to the truth of what transpired. For already the boy was shaking his crumpled clothes, getting himself into some sort of shape to face the street.

"Your parents ... are they ...?"

"In ... St.," he stated bluntly.

"Some bread," they said, sensing his hunger. They watched him chewing on it and knew he had not eaten, possibly for several days.

"Go in peace, my boy," they said simply, and it sounded almost like a benediction.

"You too, Aunt Chaya and Cousin Sonia — and may you find whomever you are looking for," he said, looking back for a last time at the two slight, sharp-eyed women, never guessing that they would. Ultimately Sonia was spared and eventually settled in Los Angeles and Aunt Chaya survived the maelstrom, carrying the distinct label 'Schindlerfrau' to her quiet grave in Bnei Brak.

"So, now that you were released from the attic, how did you feel?"

"Relieved, certainly. I was not going to die here after all. I would rejoin the family. But I knew that that was not the end of the story, We jumped from one dangerous situation to another in those days. We were never liberated from fear. I knew I would go now from this attic hideout to my parents' hiding place. I did not know what I would find there."

Reunited With His Parents

The boy turned homeward. He walked quickly down the main street, filling his lungs with the uncustomary sharpness of the air. His steps retraced earlier journeys between his home and that of his grandfather, but the past failed to hold him now, as it had while lying listless in the attic during those slow-moving hours. On the street, one lived for the present, for that is all one possessed with any surety. The next moment might well find one lying dead in the gutter, brains blown out by a bored SS man seeking to enliven his day a little.

Reaching the familiar brownstone apartment, he knocked in the agreed manner. His heart skipped a beat, two beats. The door opened. His father's figure, his mother behind him, sisters, brothers.

"Is it you my boy?"

His father's fingers grazed his cheek lightly, questioningly, as if to assure himself that this was his son, and not some vivid specter of his imagination.

"You are alright? We feared —" and his voice tailed off soundlessly, not saying what it was they had feared.

"I am fine," he said, with the intuitive carelessness of youth. "Now, tell me, what has been happening?"

Visit to Chrzanow

We reached a certain point in my father's story, but then we were not following any particular chronological order. He was telling his story, jumping backwards and forwards in time, and I was listening. At a certain point, we stopped by mutual

Our house on Jagielonska Street

agreement, and decided that now was the time for me to go to Poland. I had been pushing off doing this, but my father had been urging me. "When will you go? It would be different if you went. You would understand it all better." So, one day, I simply booked my ticket and boarded a plane.

I reached Cracow by train from Warsaw, and then hired a taxi to Chrzanow. By this time I was in a daze. The words: "It all exists ..." hammered through my brain, like a dull refrain. "It is still here."

But Chrzanow itself? Chrzanow was to me a kind of fairyland, a Chelm peopled by sages and simpletons. Chrzanow was sacred, embalmed in the realms of mythology. How could I go to Chrzanow and simply walk its streets? It would be like taking a pleasure cruise on the Red Sea! And could I go to Chrzanow without Father?

The first thing I noticed when I got out of the taxi was that Chrzanow is fairly nondescript, and in parts a modern town. I was trembling. People were walking around, Poles dressed in up-to-date attire, shopping or returning from work. They were simply going about their daily business, unconcerned about genocide, Jews, or pogroms. For time, of course, had played a vanishing trick and there was nothing here to see — nothing that was 'quick' and 'alive' in the Jewish sense. Everything was dead and inanimate — trees, buildings, cobblestones, winding streets, river.

It was a larger town than I had imagined, hardly a shtetl. Indeed, some of the streets were broad, tree-lined boulevards in the continental mode. I found myself on Krakowska Street, which runs like a great pulsing artery from the heart of the rynek (marketplace). I followed the road for a further ten or fifteen minutes. It bent and undulated, the houses becoming less and less frequent, until I reached the river and the open countryside. This was a spot father had often spoken of, the Piaski (Sand), for it was here on lazy Shabbos afternoons that the cream of Chrzanow youths would gather. I slid down the sandy banks, and sat for a moment or two in the clearing, hat in hand, under the hot Polish sun. "Look and listen," Father had briefed me, "and if you are patient, the past will come to you, and you will see the Chrzanow of my youth." This was what I now awaited, the past in all its frightening wholeness, the bittersweet, secondhand memories, brittle and crackling, like autumn leaves.

A group of chassidic boys — perhaps 11 or 12, earlocked, shirts white, lovingly starched — now stirred into life at one end of the sands. Their slim, mischievous figures darted here and there in perpetual motion. Then, all at once, they were sitting, grouped around an older boy or leader. Words of Torah intermingled with summer sounds, the gentle lapping of water on the shore, the shrill bird cries: "Torah iz die bester sechoirah — Torah is the best merchandise."

Over and over again, this vibrant refrain was heard. Yes, this surely was the past. But which of all these pale, cheder faces, newly tinged by the sun, belonged to Father?

The varying strands of Chrzanow youth which came to the 'Sand' kept firmly apart, like concentric circles, skimming but never touching. This, Father had told me. So at the farther reaches of the sands, backed by trees, I saw groups of youngsters representing various strata of Chrzanow society — Bundists, Communists, Maccabee Sports Club. Some dashed laughingly in and out of the sparkling cold waters, while others strolled, heads down, talking perhaps of politics or literature, seeing nothing but their dream, their future which stretched out before them, beckoning in all its brightly tinseled elusiveness.

After a while, I tired of the 'Sand' and its ghosts, and retraced my steps, jacket slung over my shoulder.

Now that I had seen the past resurrect itself, I was sure that I could repeat this 'trick of light' over and over again in any Chrzanow location I chose.

But at this realization, a terrible sadness at once took hold of me. If the past could indeed be brought to life, if it was so

real, so brown, so solid,
then the stabbing pain of
the irretrievable loss was a-
thousandfold sharper. For it
was not only here that was
the fact of the matter. This
entire living world was
gone, and only its hot
breath remained on my
face. It was only, after all,
time dancing its perennial
teasing dance, time with
clay on both its hobnailed
boots. While these thoughts
occurred to me with
quickening alacrity, I was

Reifer family Residence

actually walking back into the town, and subconsciously my
feet must have led me through the fashionable quarter and out
the other side. I did not know how long I walked in this way,
my eyes squinted up against the hard, dimensionless glare of
the sun. It may have been an hour, perhaps more. Passersby
glanced curiously at me, for to the inhabitants of modern
Chrzanow, a traditionally garbed Jew was an anachronism.
Fifty years ago, my appearance would have not drawn these
curious stares.

At last, looking up, footsore and out of breath, I saw that
the past had led me to the Jewish quarter, and its poor crooked
streets. But here, unlike at the Piaski, I had no initial difficulty
in realizing the past. On the contrary, impressions simply
crowded in on me, screamed at me like bystanders at the scene
of an accident, yelling to be let in. From every nook and
cranny, every cobblestoned lane, every courtyard, the life of
the place pulsated. Bewigged women staggered under heavy
burdens, boys ran and tripped each other on their way to
cheder, braided adolescent girls grouped chattering in

whispers, mothers scolded, teachers chided. Sounds of Torah emanated from every dwelling, from the humblest to the most spacious, for the place was literally soaked with traditions and the ancient living ways. The delicious spicy aromas of the Sabbath mingled with the odors of marketday and rotting fruit, and the smell of kerosene lamps. Clotheslines fluttered in breezes like proud sentinels, and sounds of mats being shaken out on a hundred balconies assailed the quickening air. If this was Chrzanow, I thought, this was a thousand Jewish communities, twinkling like stars in the Jewish constellation, a thousand shtetlach, all 'almonds and raisins,' all foul dust and sweetened aromas, all abortive sorrows as old as exile, and summer dreams, dreamed under other skies. Branching off a side street, my father had told me, there was a square courtyard that had been his favorite playground. Here, he had raced and spun and wheeled, played leap-frog and hide-and-seek, while his mother waited several streets away in the narrow apartment, dinner drying out on the stove, her patience wearing thin as sandpaper. Crossing the narrow street after a rainstorm was like crossing the Red Sea. On the other hand, Krzyska Street inspired a feeling of terror. A long, winding street, it was here that funeral processions would not infrequently make their way. Tsabanes (Christians) lived on the street, and to the children of the self-imposed ghetto, this fact alone would be enough to inspire a shivering dread.

Next, I located my father's house, a simple brownstone apartment building. The peeling façade suggested decay and disrepair. I might knock and gain entrance, for there were signs of habitation. But something held me back, for I stood on as if rooted to the spot. Not a few feet away now, I knew lay the cellar where father and a dozen others had watched in dread, on a particular ghetto afternoon. I knew the story so well that it ran in parallel grooves in my brain.

✺✺✺

There had been twelve of them, twelve of them squeezed underground into the airless cellar. On this occasion, father had been with them. The shouting had begun a few streets away. It had drawn nearer. In the cellar — silence, only the sharp intake of their breaths. But they were here now apparently, in the building. They had started from the top. The steady knock of hammers on the wall, on ceilings, on any miserable hollowed-out place marked their progress. Was ever any animal in the wild hunted with such zeal or ferocious cunning?

"They are here! We are done for, done for," a neighbor whispered in panic. Someone put a hand over her mouth. Her words hung like unanswered question marks in the foul-smelling air. Next came a new sound, just above them. The floorboards, they had found the loose ones and were patiently prying them open. First daylight flowed in unexpectedly as one board was removed, and then a torch shone directly into their widened eyes. At this Mr. ... bolted from his place, like a frightened hare, springing towards the opening.

"Well, well, and what have we here?" the German had laughed good humoredly. "Now for the other rats. My G-d, the Jews are sprouting from the earth. Now one, two, three, four." Feet placed firmly apart, he continued to smile and count. It had been, after all, a good day's work, and he had every cause for satisfaction.

Shmuel Reifer's father, newly hauled out of the cellar, stood trembling on the ground floor of his apartment, next to his daughter, an adolescent girl of 15 or 16. She was dark-haired, pale, with finely chiseled features. Now, she cowered next to her father. The German raised his rifle. At that moment, Shmuel Reifer screamed. He fell to the floor and lay there for all the world like a lifeless corpse.

"Don't touch him," one of the Germans screamed. "Leave him, he is finished!" and he kicked him once just for good measure.

"Now, to more important business. That chicken in the other room," he continued, "who supplied it?" he addressed the young girl.

"I do not know."

"Where did you get that chicken?" he lashed out wildly, kicking her and tearing her hair. "Tell us, tell us, what monkey business is going on here! We will know!"

Shmuel Reifer stirred. The shouting and kicking had dislodged the conscious part of his brain. He saw where he was, and what was transpiring. In a flash, he was on his feet, out through the opened window, and running, running, his sister's terror-stricken eyes persistently transmitting their signals: "Now Shmuel, take your chance. Be gone, be gone."

> *In fact it was this story that stayed my hand, and prevented me from knocking on the door. For I had seen the airless cellar, and before that the comfortable living room, the narrow scullery, in my mind's eye a thousand times. If I knocked and was shown around, by some uncomfortable Polish factory worker and his wife, the new reality would displace these images. No, surely it was clearer to me and more real from the pavement. I stood for a moment digesting this simple truth and watching the sun set in great swatches of oranges and reds behind the Jewish quarter.*
>
> *Everything, it was true, was still here. The only thing missing was us Jews. I felt somehow emptied, swept clean of all emotions. There was no pain, no despair, no hope, but simply nothingness, a feeling of blankness where the past had been. The remainder of my pilgrimage passed like the dead clicking of a camera, as it soundlessly recorded images. I saw everything, and stored it all away in some neat compartment of my brain. At the cemetery, long overgrown, I asked for the key from a surly old Pole. He seemed surprised to see a live Jew, as if all the Jews had been relegated long ago to some vast universal cemetery.*

The interior of the fomer Reifer residence, 1999. The Riefers' furniture is still there.

"From where you are coming?" he asked, fixing me in a toothless stare.

"England."

"England! There are zhids in England?!" he muttered, "Well, well, what is the world coming to!" and he shuffled ahead.

The afternoon passed in wearisome fashion, and he was glad when he had finished, and could decently take his leave. The ill-tended cemetery, the overgrown grass and neglected tombstones, the bad-tempered cemetery attendant, all seemed like some overstated hyperbole. The old Pole was right, a live Jew was an anachronism, something to wonder at, for the whole of Poland was a cemetery. If you wanted to cry, there were better places to do it. You could stand and weep at the

Grave of my great-great-grandfather,
R' Elyakim Getzel Reifer

Grave of my grandfather and namesake, R' Shmuel Reifer

Grave of the Rav, Rav Naftali Halberstam

Mass grave of 37 Jews killed by the Nazis

sky, noticing the faint billowing of smoke from a thousand chimneys, or let your tears drip into the earth while sifting the dry, gravelly soil through your fingers and still after all these years, uncovering human bones. Yes, indeed, there were far better places to cry.

The rynek (marketplace) was one of the last places I visited. It was a typical cobblestoned affair, flanked by three-story buildings. It was empty except for a babushka-clad flower seller in one corner. The stems of the purplish flowers she displayed were plunged into buckets of ice-cold water to keep them from drying out. Occasionally, as she let out her intricately worded cry, the water splashed in vaguely purplish puddles on the cobblestones. In this marketplace, my father should have seen the cowed mass of Jews waiting for deportation, but instead he saw a more recent image. He had come back here shortly after the war had ended, and in this very marketplace my father had been sold a pound of apples wrapped in the pages of a Gemara.

"What are you doing?!" he had cried out as the fellow tore pages from

from the Talmud as nonchalantly as though he were dismantling a telephone directory. "Use some other paper! These are holy texts."

The vendor had chuckled aloud.

"It is perfectly good paper as I see it. Find me some other and I'll use it!"

This is the final image I saw as I lingered for a while in the Chrzanow marketplace. That and the sight of a solitary sycamore tree in the infamous Henkier Platz. Was this the same tree on which the Germans had hanged seven hostages in April 1942, among them Gerstner, Waldman and Szpangelet? Of this, there was a faded snapshot in circulation, for a casual eyewitness had recorded the scene. In faded black and white, one could make out the figure of the German demi-god, hands behind his back, regarding his handiwork, and three rag-doll black-clad figures, necks broken, dangling from the cleverly improvised gallows.

Back in England

"Father, I went to Poland ... But somehow, it is more real to me here."

"That is how I felt the first time I returned after the war in a truck filled with survivors. I felt emptied out, bereaved all over again. I had come back to something which, for all intents and purposes, no longer existed. Somehow, the fact that it still existed in a physical sense made it worse. It was an audacity for the familiar streets to have remained unharmed. Everything was still there. There was only one thing missing: US. And nobody cared! Nobody mourned us. We were not real people. We were luftmenschen, comprised of nothing more substantial than air. We could be blown away. We had been blown away. Some of the gentiles looked at us with unabashed hatred, as if to say: 'Go back to the dead. You have no right to breathe, to

occupy space, to come back here as if you own the place.'

"You sometimes ask me why I am a little cynical of human nature. Well, I have found out, to my detriment, that people are fickle creatures. They will do and say what suits them, what is convenient for them at that particular moment — even people who are of seemingly high principles. This I learned from our long-time neighbors, the Poles, with whom we lived in proximity for hundreds of years, if not always coexisting peacefully, at least living side by side. We did business with them, employed them or were employed by them, rubbed shoulders on trams, but when it came to the crunch, there were so few, pitifully few, who shed a tear for us, let alone tried to help us. No, they turned their back in that peculiarly Polish way, shrugging their shoulders, shutting their eyes and ears, hearing, seeing, saying ... nothing."

Hanging of the Seven

Life in the ghetto was never, and could never be, the same after the 'Hanging of the Seven.' It became qualitatively different. This was the desired effect, for the seven 'criminals' had been arrested on blatantly trumped-up charges, which ranged from being sus- pected of operating a bakery without due permission, to possess- ing a shriveled-up quarter of a sausage. This is just how far reach- ing the tentacles of the new world order were in Poland of 1942. Shmuel Reifer was one of those whose personal documents had been taken away from him. These would only be returned to their owners on attendance at the Henkier Platz for what was advertised all over the ghetto by Germans, riding megaphoned trucks, as 'an interesting and educational spectacle.' Thus, it transpired that he was standing on that April day in the midst of a crowd of his dejected fellow Jews. This was nothing less than a parody of an enjoyable, peacetime spectacle. The Germans arrived dressed in their best uniforms, with wives or fiances, and all in the best humor, for they insisted that the event was a festivity. It seemed that the 'bigwigs' had turned out for the occasion for, in addition Commandant Schindler, the chief of police, the chief of Gestapo, Dreher from Katowice was visible in the front row. However, noticeably, for such a 'festive' event, the spectators did not crane their necks to get a 'better view.'

"Eyes ahead," a German officer spat out in sneering fashion. "After all, you do not want to miss anything."

The Germans moved swiftly among the miserable crowd, ensuring this very end. With a lash of a rifle butt in a strategically aimed blow, they soon had all the Jews fixing their eyes on the sycamore trees ahead. Is it possible to look and not see? Observe and not retain images? For this is what the Jews of Chrzanow now proceeded to do.

The seven were brought in, among them the baker Gerstner and his two sons, Shaya Szpangelet and the others, more dead than alive. Meanwhile, seven qualified hangmen had been imported for the occasion. The Germans in the front rows continued to beam in a mixture of triumph and disdain. The spectacle lasted for two hours —two hours in which each of the seven screamed out *"Shema Yisroel"* and *"Yidden, nekamah* — avenge our blood." With these words on their lips they strangled to death in front of the assembled cross-section of Chrzanow Jewry.

Henkier Platz - monument to the seven who were hanged there

Shmuel Reifer was remembering these final ghetto days as one remembers the death throes of an animal, thrashing in agony. From the blackness of this pit, this garbage heap, it was now possible, if thinking was at all possible, to see it all in its true perspective. All those final events which they had thought so horrific, so ominous, were in fact only aspects of a diabolical Grand Design. In themselves, they had no true finality. How they had wondered at them, how they had discussed, hour after hour, their true significance.

"They will hang seven of us as a warning, but then our troubles will lessen. This will be the last atrocity of its kind." They talked too, of resettlement, a better life to the East. Then there was the talk of resettlement to Lodz ghetto! There were many who, falling for this last lie, wanting desperately to believe, bartered their remaining valuables to get on transports leaving supposedly to the ghetto of Lodz. Chrzanow Jews were joined by neighboring Jews from Sosnowice, and together they gathered at the appointed hour. Curiously, hope was still lodged in their hearts. Somehow, it had survived after months of ghetto hell. They had scrambled onto the waiting trains. Needless to say, the trains did not stop at neighboring Lodz. The great lie continued to haunt them in its varying forms. But the aforementioned, surprisingly endless capacity for hope not only kept them alive, it also, of course, simultaneously drove them towards their deaths, as surely as the wheels of the trains turned in their inevitable chugging rhythm.

These were the generalities, but more detailed memories occupied the youth's mind. He remembered, for example, the strange aftermath of the day on which he had fled from his cellar hideout, his sister's eyes speeding him on his way. He had been discovered by the policeman, Lenz, in a cousin's home where he had fled. He was still dazed and in some level of confusion and fear. The SS man, Lenz, finding the semi-comatose boy shouted: "Stay here. I will come back and decide what to do with you both."

Of course, as soon as his uniformed back was out of sight, Shmuel took leave of his cousin and darted out, back onto the street, and made his way homewards. Strangely enough, his father and sister were at home. For some reason their SS man had also stalked off, leaving them there in total confusion. The matter of the chicken had apparently remained unresolved. Such was the

German method in madness. On that day, however, the SS 'pickings' had been unusually rich. One hundred and fifty Jews had been caught in the net, including the president of the Judenrat, Mr. Zucker, and his assistants, Mr. Nussbaum and Mr. Teichler. Even Mr. Laderer, who was classified as a *nizliche Jude* (a Jew needed for the war effort), and who with his wife had cooperated fully with the Gestapo, dealing in foreign currencies, was arrested on that day. Within our immediate family, an aunt and cousin had been deported. None of these people were ever heard from again.

However, these were the early days, and one glorious Chrzanow summer day a consignment of boxes arrived at the Judenrat. Shmuel had gone there that day, to sort out some problem with his card. Neat, labeled boxes stood in the hallway, blocking the entire entranceway. Everyone was standing, as if transfixed to the spot, eyes rooted to the strange orderly pile.

"What does it mean?" he had nudged the fellow standing next to him, a tall, spare-looking man who kept pushing his glasses nervously back onto his nose.

"Ashes," the man kept saying. "These are ashes. We will have to pay one hundred and twenty marks for these ashes." Then he added as an afterthought: "The price has gone up!"

Chrzanow's Liquidation

Another major *Aktion* had taken place, located at the infamous Henkier Platz. On February 18, 1943, the ghetto had been completely surrounded with German Police and SS units. In this very 'thorough' operation, the Germans had gone from house to house, 'flushing out' their prey and rounded them up at the Henkier Platz. In one particular cellar, they had 'flushed out' forty Jews. At this discovery, so incensed were the members of the 'Master Race' that they wished to shoot these forty on the spot. However, the well-known Moishe Marin, who held considerable sway with the Germans, had intervened at the last moment, strutting up in his self-important manner, and actually proceeded to beg for mercy. As a gesture of clemency the Germans had allowed them to join the other three thousand Jews who were assembled at the Henkier Platz. With what relief they greeted relatives and friends in the crowd!

"Moishe Marin intervened on our behalf. They let us go, they let us go."

In any event, it turned out that all they had been spared from, like mice scurrying back and forth in an intricate maze, was a quick death, in return for one which was mercilessly drawn out.

The end for Chrzanow Jewry, when it had come, had come in so many differing guises, but from this new vantage point it was possible to see that these were all nothing but variations on a theme. There had been those who, near the beginning, had been sent to Siberia. Here they were dumped, not imprisoned, in the midst of a veritable desert of ice, and told to build their own accommodations. There was nothing for them but to try to fell the huge timbers and construct a shelter of sorts. They soon discovered that for nine months of the year the temperature remained at fifty degrees below zero. They were given further incentives to work well, for they were promised a pair of boots after a year of labor, and after another year, a heavy, waterproof anorak. However, it was necessary for them to survive until that point, on the most meager of rations, and survival without boots and an outer covering was, at any rate, a precarious matter.

Yet another group of five hundred from Chrzanow were taken east and dressed as railway workers. Under the supervision of the Romanian military command, they were set to work. They were put to sleep in unheated railroad cars and given no water whatsoever. The bread, when it arrived, was frozen and virtually inedible. The work consisted of broadening the gauge of the railway tracks, so that German trains could pass directly to the front.

Added to malnutrition and horrendous conditions, typhus then struck. After three months of this treatment, barely one hundred of the original number of healthy young men remained alive.

But the *Moloch* was insatiable. Contrary to expectations, however, after many were dispatched east or west to unknown destinations, the demands did not cease but grew ever more outrageous. If one hundred were demanded one day, it was two hundred on the next. If the numbers were not filled, wives were held as hostages for husbands, children for parents.

When on a certain notable occasion, three hundred girls between the ages of 18 and 25 were demanded through the agency of the Judenrat, and only one hundred and fifty showed up, Marin sent in an inspector. Commissar Mayerovitch, acting directly on Moishe Marin's orders, attempted to explain to the terrified ghetto dwellers that if orders were not complied with and the girls handed over, entire families would be sent to Auschwitz. The mention of the mysterious name 'Auschwitz,' which until the war broke out had portended nothing more sinister than their neighboring town, was generally sufficient to win the argument. Shmuel Reifer's sister was among those on the list. She had not gone originally, but when her mother was taken in her place and news reached the family that she had been put to work in snow and ice, the daughter, with a profound sigh, being unable to bear the thought of her delicate mother suffering in her place, went herself.

In another instance, eight hundred Chrzanow boys were taken. This had been near the beginning. They were detained in the schoolhouse for a week, while some, sensing their doom was at hand, attempted to escape. They were taken to a camp called Sakrow, in Upper Silesia. Here they were housed in empty barracks. There was no actual task to complete, but they were placed under the direction of the SA who did all they could to embitter their young lives. After a while, they were put to work felling forests. This was dangerous work for unskilled young men, as one false stroke of the axe could bring about their death.

And so it continued.

The Death Camp of Auschwitz

"Did it not finally become clear to you that something more terrible than the sum of these individual things was at hand?"

"I suppose that to this generation we must now appear rather shortsighted. But what you must remember is that we were working on assumptions without precedent, perhaps in all of human history. Massacres, pogroms, we might anticipate, even mass slaughter, but genocide? To systematically and cold heartedly plan the destruction of an entire nation, that no one, not even a prophet could have envisaged. You know that it was all done, too, in such a methodical way. To this day this is still to me the most incredible aspect of it all. Oswiciem was the Polish name for Auschwitz. It was our neighboring town, a very pleasant community of staunchly Orthodox Jews. It was only eighteen kilometers from Chrzanow, a journey of some ten or fifteen minutes by train. Later, when the infamous death camp of Auschwitz was well-established, a consignment of Chrzanow Jews was due to be shipped off there. Now, as I have told you, this was a very short journey by train. But you know what they did, the Germans, they should perish? They kept them waiting for two days in the sealed boxcars. You see, the gas chambers were busy just then, and the driver had to wait for a signal from the 'higher authorities' at Auschwitz-Birkenau to let them know that a gas chamber had become free! Can you imagine? Could you ever imagine such a thing?!

"Something else. Let me tell you about the soap. Well, don't blame me. You wanted to hear it all. You told me you were ready to hear. Have you really the stomach for it?"

"Yes. I'm OK. Please, continue."

"Well, I suppose you know how the facilities worked at

Auschwitz. The central feature was the gas chambers. They were housed in low buildings with sliding iron doors and no windows. They were disguised as bathhouses. To the end, the unsuspecting victims thought that they would be taking a shower. Yes, they believed this to the very last minute. They were pushed into the room, crammed in to capacity and then the iron doors were clanged shut. The victims were inside. The gassing took twenty minutes. The floor of the gas chamber was a false floor. It was a sliding one, so that when the death process was over, the floor simply moved across and the corpses fell into waiting lorries, which sped them directly to the crematorium. (By the way, these huge crematoria were manufactured by a firm in Berlin which was proud to have the exclusive right to patent them.) Nothing was wasted. The corpses were systematically stripped, all gold teeth or crowns removed and melted down. The bones were pulverized in an enormous grinding machine, until they formed a fine yellow powder. This was then used as fertilizer in German fields. The human fat from the corpses was rendered into containers. It was allowed to solidify, and then made into bars of soap known as RIF — Rhein Israelitche Fat (Pure Jewish Fat). This too is unimaginable! But yes, we lived through these things. After the war, by the way, we buried as many of those bars of soap as we could find."

To the Left or Right

One of the final events had been the summoning of all Jews still left in the ghetto to gather at 9 a.m. to a specific assembly point. By now, such summonses were the daily fare of ghetto life, and the state of demoralization of most ghetto dwellers made compliance to this latest order relatively matter of fact. If the gray matter in the brain simply ceased functioning, refused to think any further, then looking up at an unfamiliar sky and clutching your card in a convulsive grip between your tired fingers, was the only thing that mattered. Perhaps they now felt they were inhabiting a new world which was material without being real. They were nothing but ghosts, breathing the last of their miserable dreamlike air. Now, they were divided simply into two lines, and it soon became apparent that some people's cards were being stamped 'blue' and some 'red.' The assembly point was under extremely heavy guard for it seemed that a whole division of SS from Katowice had been enlisted for the event. The familiar figures of SS men Dreher, Frietag and Kronau were visible too, milling at the front end of the square, where tables had been set up to deal with the inevitable paperwork. Now, from muttered undertones, it became apparent that there was consternation spreading like contagion among the waiting Jews. What do the blue or red stamps portend? Who could be called lucky, who unlucky, for there was no immediate way of telling? One of Shmuel Reifer's last memories of Chrzanow was standing on a low wall behind the assembled mass, noticing that those in the right-hand line were being marched off in looser, less tight-knit fashion than those to the left. He had there and then made a snap decision. He would advise his family to try and get into the right-hand line.

No, the end had not come on that day, for the move to the right-hand line had, after all, proved to be a fortuitous one. They had been marched slowly around the streets and then simply released. But 'release' from an unknown hell, back into a known one, can hardly be termed release. With such 'illusions' of 'luck' and 'escape,' ghetto dwellers lived until the end. But of one thing everybody was now certain with a new and terrible certainty — his turn would come. After this 'escape,' Shmuel Reifer knew that his days in Chrzanow were numbered. This was because the realization had now come to them that their situation was impossible.

They had no food, no connections. It was only a matter of time before the Germans would discover their cellar hideout. It had been discovered once already. They decided to leave Chrzanow and try their luck in a neighboring village. Accordingly, he, his brother and father had walked to the station and boarded a train. They had done this separately so as not to arouse attention, for this action in the Poland of 1943 was no less than audacious. If they were recognized by any stray policemen or by their neighbors, death would not be far behind. Covering their yellow stars with their tattered jackets, they held their breaths.

The train spluttered to life and then simply stopped. Everyone in the carriage waited. A babushka-clad Polish peasant woman seated in one corner was muttering words of prayer or imprecation. Babies in arms cried. One or two Polish soldiers stood and smoked, leaning their heads out the window. In that single moment in the shabby compartment with wooden seats, waiting for the proposed journey to begin, a pain, more piercingly human than any since it had all begun, had stabbed the youth through and through. For there were really people who still pursued a mundane life, conducted business, raised their children, went to church on Sundays, traveled to neighboring villages, and yet they — as Jews — were as effectively excluded from that world as if they were aliens from another planet.

At that moment, the train's wheels started to turn, and the conductor, with his roll of tickets, began to pass through the carriages. The train drew into Sosnowice. There, they alighted as planned. It seemed to him momentarily that the stationmaster was eyeing him with a sharpening glint of recognition. Recognition was possible here, for he and his brother had often traveled to Sosnowice on errands for their father. The only thing to do now was to walk in as unconcerned a manner as possible. So they walked on and on, not stopping to look back or even to draw breath, until they had entered the ghetto's main streets. Here they had furtively removed their jackets, dropped their tense expressions and mingled with the crowd.

Sosnowice

Sosnowice, however, proved not to be a safe haven. On the contrary, it was a veritable hell where starvation, privation, despair and death stalked the streets. Deportations were frequent. Unbelievably, conditions here might even be described as worse than in Chrzanow. Finding a roof over their heads was problematic, but after some searching, an elderly shoemaker admitted them to his cramped surroundings.

On the first evening, turning to the youth, he had said quietly:

"Look here, young man, can you see what's going on here? Why don't you run away to the forests and join the partisans? You will certainly have a better chance than remaining in the ghetto!"

Shmuel looked up as these words were spoken, and his eyes met those of his father. His father, who had once been so trim and upright, now looked haggard and desperately unkempt. But worse, in his gray eyes there was a despair which signaled to the boy that he was walking an unseen tightrope. He was just managing to retain his sanity in a world grown dark and incomprehensible. If his eldest son were to walk out on him now, he would simply let go of this tenuous grip. He would slip away, because he would no longer have the will to hold on. All these thoughts passed through the boy's mind in rapid succession, like the staccato pitter-patter of a rifle. And in those seconds, too, came his decision. He would stay whatever happened.

Surprisingly, the next plan of action came at the prompting of the boy's father. General Schneldt had Germanized the Polish farms that were scattered throughout the German sector of Poland. Here, German nationals were to run the farms, and Jews were imported as cheap labor. Shmuel's father, who still had several diamonds in his possession, decided that the time was now ripe to make use of them. To wait any longer would be futile. Handing them over to his 'connection,' who would then pass them over to the SS, he experienced twinges of regret, as if he were cutting loose the last of his lifeboats. However, this was only a momentary feeling, and it passed in an instant. He realized only too clearly the full precariousness of their position here in Sosnowice. However, it was still a great risk, for he had no way of gauging the reliability of his contact. It was fully within the realm of possibility that the diamonds would be handed over, and nothing done in exchange to help them. The next morning, however, an SS man approached them, clicking his heels smartly. He had come, he said in precise manner, to escort: *"Drei stüng Jüden zur arbeit."*

The work on the now germanized Polish farm was hard, but not unbearable. These men, by now veterans of German forced labor squads, saw that there was a distinctly noticeable difference in degree. There were other more tangible benefits, too. For one thing, the 'Death's Head' was not present, and that represented a real psychological benefit. They felt themselves to be more free, more at ease. The food was far more plentiful. There were potatoes to be had and sour milk. The three ghetto dwellers felt as if they had fallen into paradise, but simultaneously they knew that this could not last, would prove to be only a temporary reprieve. Something infinitely worse, more hellish, the reality of their ghetto-filled nightmares must necessarily be just around the corner.

"This was a kind of respite. I suppose you sensed that it could not last."
"True, nothing in those days was permanent. We were like animals on the run, escaping from one trap, only to fall into another. But the end was at hand, if not tomorrow, then the

day after or the day after that. We all knew that, sensed it in our bones. No Jew was safe on the face of Europe. And this is where the notorious Obersturmführer Linde turns up again in my story."

Obersturmführer

Obersturmführer Linde's days were filled with activity. But the 'task' which the Germans had set themselves was so large, so awesome, that on some days he would experience lapses of uncertainty. Could it be done? Could it ever finally be achieved? However, these lapses were rare, and time for reflection of this kind was limited, for each day brought new challenges. The letters he wrote home to his wife were full of oblique references to "pride at our great achievement, even though at times, great courage is needed to carry out our appointed task." Linde tended to think of himself as a 'roving ambassador,' ready to travel to the ends of the earth to further the glorious end of his masters. But the 'enemy' was cunning! Oh, so filled with cunning! And the more he confronted this almost subhuman quality, the more he became convinced of the essential rightness of their aims. Many were the 'search and destroy' missions that he was ordered to embark on. These missions were 'Jew hunts' (Jüdenjagd), with all the almost pleasurable, adventurous, connotations of that word. But the 'hunter' had to possess a single-minded level of dedication to the task. Nothing less would do. Having already participated in countless 'mopping-up operations,' Linde felt himself to be well-experienced in these matters. It was with a slight sense of déjà vu, therefore, that he departed from Chrzanow one August night in 1943, his destination a German-run farm near Sosnowice. Here, it was reported, a sizeable number of Jews had managed to infiltrate and gain employment.

It was a hot Polish night. Linde, stepping out of his official car, mopped the droplets of sweat which had formed on his brow. Night work, even though it necessitated leaving his comfortable bed and fine duvet, had a certain thrill about it, which was undeniable. It was as if the events gained more depth, more significance than those perpetrated by day. At once, he gave orders for the farm to be completely surrounded by his men. There would be no means of escape. Next, he issued specific orders for everyone, from the lowliest farmhand to the farm owners, to gather in front of the largest barn. They came one by one, disheveled, bleary-eyed. They formed a miserable, ragged assembly, urged by his men to stand in some sort of formation. He scanned the assembled mass, and let the silence, which had now dropped like an unseen menace from the darkened sky, work its terror. This was an oft-tried and trusted method. In those seconds, continuing to glance over the faces, he could tell, almost at sight, who were the Jews. It was something 'hunted' in the look, which no amount of self-control could subdue. But it took a well-trained eye to detect this. Next, turning to the farm owner, who was standing stiffly at attention, only a slight tremor in his eye betraying his nervousness, Linde called out: "*Wievil stünk Jüden?* (How many foul-smelling Jews?)"

The reply came, and the figure more or less tallied with his mental estimates. The corner of his mouth lifted in the slightest movement of self-satisfaction.

"Is there anyone left in the farm buildings?"

Silence.

He turned to his second in command. "Conduct a thorough search of the buildings. If you find anyone there, shoot to kill."

Five, ten minutes elapsed. The air was thick with silence. One expected at any moment to hear the quick peppering of shots. Apparently, his men had had no luck.

Next, he called out: "Send for the *Bürgermeister* of this village immediately!"

"But sir," the underling had protested. "It is 3 in the morning."

"No matter. Bring him here, and on the double."

The car's engine throttled, then purred into a slow movement.

"We wait," he said, almost to himself, forgetting for a moment the dozens of haunted eyes riveted on his clear-cut features.

Minutes ticked by. Finally, the car was heard in the distance, again as if all the night's variegated sounds were concentrated on that one sound.

The *Bürgermeister*, still confused, tumbled out of the car, striving to retain some vestige of his customary dignity.

"Are you the *Bürgermeister* of this town?" Linde snapped.

"Yes."

"This place is being liquidated of its Jews immediately. I hand over this responsibility to your administration and I expect a full accounting by tomorrow afternoon."

At this, with a flicker of his cold eyes to his men, and a scant sardonic glance to those still standing in the tense night air, awaiting a sign of what their fate would be, he turned smartly on his heels and departed.

The March to Klobuck

For the rest of his life, Shmuel Reifer would never forget the next few days, or what transpired in the course of them. Following Linde's summary departure and his curt orders, the *Bürgermeister* had, somewhat reluctantly, taken charge. It was finally decided, after a roll-call had been taken and the Jews firmly moved to one side, to march them off in the direction of Klobuck, where the nearest police station was located. Darkness was already beginning to give way to dawn, as pearly streaks spread like timid fingers across the sky. In addition to this, birdsong was now heard, the daily dawn chorus, but this did little to lift their spirits. In fact, it almost seemed to them that these cheerful humdrum sounds mocked them, in all the futile desperation of their situation. They had been on their feet all night and now the march to Klobuck seemed endless. Every bend in the road was a cruel prolonging of their torture. Finally, they walked as if they were automatons, their feet obeying, but not their brains. Some deep residual instinct told them that to stay alive it was necessary to put one foot in front of another.

In Klobuck, they were herded into the yard of the police station and left there. At first this proved a welcome relief from the walking, for they could now sit or crouch or lie on the concrete. But as soon as night began to fall and it became obvious that they were not being offered any type of shelter, food or drink, their spirits plumetted again. A noise like a low, strangled sob broke from them, such as might issue from an animal in its death throes. No distinct words were articulated. Sleep finally fell upon them, as they lay bone-weary on the unyielding stone. No sooner had their eyes closed, it seemed to them, than they awoke, drenched in sweat, limbs aching, to the unflinching reality of the gray yard, the concrete, the forbidding building. In this way time passed in the yard, with each day bringing new arrivals. Now even a little space in which to stretch one's limbs became a luxury. Men and women were segregated so that families could no longer offer each other customary mutual support. On about the fifth or sixth day, a family of partisans arrived. Major Ludwig, who was in charge of this operation, was a quiet-mannered man who would speak to his charges in almost polite tones. His 'handling' of the partisan family was characteristic. He gave courteous sounding orders that they be so kind as to relocate into the police station itself. An hour later, shots rang out in the dreary afternoon.

On the seventh day, it rained. The rain fell in buckets, drenching the remains of their clothes, in which they had been standing, sitting and lying for six days and six nights. Some opened their mouths to allow the rain to fall directly onto their parched tongues.

By the eighth day it became apparent that this was an extremely thorough operation, and that the whole area had been combed for 'stray' Jews. Jews arrived from Katowice, from Sosnowice, and finally from Chrzanow itself. From the latter, one hundred and fifty Jews arrived in the final hours in the police yard. It was rumored that there were only eight Jews left in Chrzanow, for those working in the uniform factory and the soup kitchen had finally been rounded up.

In fact, Chrzanow had now been pronounced by its mayor as *Judenrein*. This effectively put an end to centuries of Jewish settlement, culture and co-existence with their neighbors. The mayor had added, almost as an afterthought, his satisfaction at this quite remarkable turn of events.

> *"I always make the same observation about the years that were to follow, as we entered the throbbing heart of the Nazi death machine, and its most symbolic institution, the 'lager' (camp). I would say that in all the lagers, which I had the misfortune to pass through, the rules or defining features were essentially one and the same. I would sometimes imagine a special office in Berlin, labeled: 'Jews: special treatment' — but failing to call itself the 'Bureau for Genocide' — in which gray-haired bureaucrats would sit on winter afternoons.*
>
> *"Did they list the transportation in cattle cars, which was the first rite of initiation into this new world? Then the shock treatment on arrival, the immediate selections, the barbarous shavings? 'Gehinnom' one might simply conceive of as being just this. One is stripped naked, sent into a shower room, forbidden to sit down. After the showering and the tattooing, one is issued prison clothing. All this seemed to be the product of one prevailing school of thought. Many of us had been dragged less than twenty-four hours previously from our own beds, but by now we were unrecognizable. Our striped pajamas had no pockets as if to prove that now we possessed and owned nothing. We were 'less' than nothing.*
>
> *"This was typical German rectitude. This rectitude manifested itself from the moment we passed under the huge sardonic sign: 'Arbeit Macht Frei — Work Makes You Free.'*

As a Jew, aware of our destiny, I did not find this altogether surprising, for pogroms, Jew hunts, blood libels were all nothing new. But the systematized ferocity of the Germans worried us. Of how many Jews did they mean to rid themselves? This was their ultimate aim, surely, and that we should live in torment until the moment of death. So death became for us the only way to break out of the 'eternal cycle,' and it was at the end of every alleyway. It lay down with us at night, its hot breath on our faces, and it woke us up in the mornings. It insinuated itself into every action carried out during the day. If we clung to life, it was something inexplicable, redolent of some primeval urge. For there was no strength left to truly think into the future, only of the next piece of bread, or the next bowl of soup."

Bautrup Nord, near Klobuck, was the first *lager* the boy and his father had the misfortune to enter. As the doors of the cattle cars opened, they knew that this was the place, or the 'thing,' that they had sensed in a bone-deep way as the Germans' ultimate purpose for them all along. All the laws, the restrictions, the movement of large segments of the populace from place to place had ultimately been aiming at this, and nothing more nor less than this. But later, as a *veteran* of the strange sub-universe of the *lagers*, the boy would come to classify this as a good camp. The food, if not plentiful, was at least enough to keep 'body and soul' together.

From Bautrup Nord they were dispatched to Blechhamer, a fairly large camp in Silesia. It contained a German chemicals plant where not only Jews but other nationals — Italians, Russians — were employed. However, it soon became apparent that here, too, the Jews were singled out for special treatment. Blechhamer fell into the category of a 'good camp' for it was clean and the food was adequate. The work, although difficult, was not unbearable. While they were at Blechhamer news reached the inmates of a personal attack on Hitler. At first euphoria swept over these prisoners, like an unstoppable tidal wave. 'Hitler attacked, possibly dead.'

Freedom could not be far off. Soon all their sufferings would pale like so many tired memories. There was a noticeably jaunty spring in the gait of the Italians and Russians, and they walked up and down by the wire, talking of what these events might mean. All that day, the SS kept to their side of the wire. They were tense and on edge. By the evening, the news leaked out. He was still alive, injured but not dead. On the receipt of this news, all the Jews in the camp were assembled and kept standing between the two wires. They were not allowed back into the camp. Hours passed in this way, with one wire behind them slicing up the sky, and one wire ahead of them.

A tall dark, gaunt figure, with hollowed-out cheeks and pock-marked skin, approached. He stepped up to the wires. This was the first sight of the *Judenhaendler* Hauschild. In fact, he was a slave-handler. He eyed the assembled mass, attentively and without malice, for he was merely sizing up a new piece of merchandise. Rolling up his sleeves, he set to work at making his selection. At once, he selected forty of the fittest young boys. These forty were told to slip out of the wires and stand quietly to one side. A crowd of about three hundred were now left between the wires. These were a mixed company of the elderly, women and the very young or the unfit. Now, SS officer Ludwig approached and entered into conversation with Hauschild. It soon became apparent from the sound of their raised voices that a fierce argument was ensuing. The three hundred between the wires looked on. The argument continued and was peppered with business terms and figures. At last, their voices fell again, became muted. Hauschild and Ludwig shook hands and saluted one another, the one tall and gaunt, the other round faced and bespectacled. A deal had been struck.

Judenhaendler Hauschild was a frequent visitor to the camp. He would arrive from time to time and haggle over a group of Jews for all the world like an accountant, making sure his figures tallied. Perhaps, in the 'real world' he had been an accountant or book-keeper, and had done nothing more malicious than offer the odd gibe to a fellow office worker while working conscientiously at his lengthy columns of figures. But he liked things to 'add up,' had a passion for it, could not bear loose ends, or details unaccounted for. Can you believe then, seeing him at work in the *lagers,* that this was the motive that drove him here to us in this transformed landscape of slaves and *untermenschen?* This is to believe in the essential ability of evil that underpinned this vast kingdom of death. For without the bureaucrats quietly adjusting their lists, making sure the numbers were right, the scientist mixing the gas to exact proportions, the manufacturers working out the exact cubic capacity of their ovens, and then setting to work day after day without fuss to assemble them, nothing of this dimension could ever have been achieved.

Judenhaendler Hauschild carried out his task of sorting and assigning with great meticulousness. Once, an epidemic broke out in the *lager.* The camp was immediately closed by the authorities, no traffic being allowed in or out — except for *Judenhaendler* Hauschild. He came, solemnly drew out his notebook, as was his wont, and with an interested eye, toured the camp, eager to see how his 'animals' behaved under these new conditions. Their various degrees of debilitation touched him, but only in their being interesting specimens. When the camp was finally declared infection-free some weeks later, Hauschild took all who had survived the infection to one side and unceremoniously shot them, thereby proving once and for all, to anyone who was still taking notes, that his interest in the Jewish problem was not merely theoretical.[2]

---

2. In Breslau after the war, Hauschild was recognized by a Jewish boy, brought to trial and sentenced to death.

From Blechhamer to Gräditz Lager

It was Hauschild too who, some months later, selected three hundred and thirty of the inmates and decided that they should be put on trains to another destination. In the trains, no matter how they huddled together, they could not get warm. Their bodies were so rundown that they gave off little heat. Nevertheless, the sealed compartments quickly became stuffy with the stale air which had nowhere to circulate, and the stench of human misery. At last, the train began to climb. The boy pricked up his nostrils. Now he could smell, through the cracks in the sides of the train, another strangely familiar smell. What was it? Oh, it was something infinitely sweet and unconnected to this world in which they now groped forward like terror-stricken nightwalkers.

"Shmuel, the pine forest," his father whispered to him. "The forests of Silesia ..." It was here in Upper Silesia that they had been accustomed to take their summer vacations, a lifetime, a universe ago. It was here, too, in these lush forests, that the trees were felled and the timber transported to the family lumberyard in Chrzanow. Triggered by these memories, a wave of melancholy swept over both the boy and his father. Surely this world could not have turned wholly black for them? Higher and higher the train rose until they cranked to a sudden stop. As the doors opened, the sign which greeted them spelled Gräditz. Was this place for life or for death? For this was how they came to rate each of their new destinations. The first landmark they passed, as they were driven forward to the now customary barking of dogs and the short whips slicing through the air, was an old-fashioned mill. This in itself signified nothing, for it seemed to them that every place and every object in the world had been utterly transformed. It was as if they were visitors from an alien planet who could not read the signs. They were forced into an empty old building, in advanced stages of decay and disrepair. It was a filthy, uninviting place, and an inauspicious beginning. Here they were left to wait. They tried sitting on the cold, dirty floor and quickly tired of that. Some of them began shifting from foot to foot, both in an attempt to keep warm and in a fit of profound unease.

The day passed, then turned into night, then into day again. At last there were noises outside the building. "Raus, raus ..." They were frog-marched forward again, on through the camp. Again, a long building, but this time there were wooden bunks, which would house three men. Of these there were several tiers, from floor to ceiling.

Appel came at 3 in the morning. They had fallen heavily into sleep, each with his own dreams of home. They then were, or so it seemed to them, physically wrenched from this haven, as illusory as a mirage in a desert, by the peculiarly low sound of the alarm. Out, out in what was, to all intents and purposes, the freezing Polish night, where in rows of five, they were counted and then recounted. Finally release, and then 'coffee' — an ersatz coffee made from chicory and several other foul-tasting ingredients — which again bore no resemblance to what they had known by that name in the free world. It had a peculiarly bitter taste which lingered in their mouths long after they had gulped the last drops down their throats.

> *Remembering, while seated in your living room, a world so utterly disparate to that which is normally viewed as the material one, is not achieved without difficulty. All that had transpired up to now had some tenuous links with a known reality, but Gräditz represented a departure. For example, there is a certain degree of guilt at having survived, as if one had somehow displaced someone else. This is common to all survivors.*
>
> *At the time, Gräditz was a culmination, too, of all of those dense, violent 'ghetto dreams,' a nightmare turned*

into reality, but also far beyond any of their wildest imaginings. Comfortably settled in Britain, many years later, he gives his son instructions about his forthcoming journey to Poland. Strangely enough it does not include exhortations to visit Gräditz or Blechhamer or any of the other black holes of that strange, inverted universe he had inhabited between the years 1939 and 1945. No, for this he tells him: "Go ask your mother. She was at Auschwitz," as if Auschwitz was the winner at the polling booth of suffering. Auschwitz is the ultimate academy. And, he adds in an undertone that is intended more for his own ears: "She may have passed me by in that submerged world. Who knows? At any rate, being from Hungary, she landed in Plazow and Auschwitz, my region of the world. And I was taken to Upper Silesia and Germany itself. There are so many unanswered questions from that time, so many things we do not understand even now."

Gräditz contained an old-fashioned mill and this was the first thing they saw as they entered the camp. It had struck them at once as a sort of symbol of country living and wholesome values. But what greeted them there did little to reinforce this primary impression. Here was nothing but dirt and squalor. That day, they had been thrust into a long, decrepit building and left to squat in the semi-darkness. They were given nothing to eat or drink. Facilities for washing were nonexistent. Eventually, they had been assigned to huts containing three tiers of wooden bunks on which were spread bundles of straw. *Appel* (roll call) in Gräditz sounded at 3 a.m. At 4:15 a.m. they were marched off to work.

In Gräditz, they were put to work building barracks. Later, the boy would come to the realization that all the work they were given was inherently useless, and usually had but one purpose: to crush their spirits and extract the last drops of humanity from them. Then, they could more easily be disposed of. Let it never be said that the Third Reich was wasteful of any resources which fell to its lot!

When Shmuel Reifer first saw the load of cement he was supposed to transport from one place to another, his heart fell. But this was impossible! No human being could be expected to carry such loads and survive. Yet, inexplicably, he proceeded to do just this. All day long, in a seemingly endless cycle, bricks, cement, cement, bricks.

"Now, at last," their supervisors goaded them, "you lazy Jews know what it is to work! You have been taught at Gräditz!"

If they stumbled or fell, they were beaten. If they stopped for a moment's pause, they were beaten. They were, for all the world, like slave laborers in Pharaoh's Egypt. And there was the realization, too, that what they were in fact building was to be their own miserable accommodations.

The beatings and severe treatment continued unabated. One gray morning, Moshe Mandlebaum, from Chrzanow, was beaten steadily by a furious kapo who had spotted him sitting on a clump of wood for a moment or two too long. Mandlebaum, a thickset, powerfully built fellow, went down without a word or a whimper. The following week, it was the turn of Shmuel Scherer from Sosnowice. A wiry youngster, he tried to resist, with a look of murderous fury in his eyes. But the consistency of the blows overcame him, and he too capitulated. He lay on the sea of mud, inert and unyielding. The kapo regarded him for a moment with something like annoyance. "The stupid thing," he seemed to enunciate. Then he kicked the 'thing' on the ground. "Bah," he eventually spat out, "he is just pretending." Taking a final aim, he strode off, cursing.

Time and time again, in so many little ways, the realization crossed the boy's mind in Gräditz that this must be the worst that they could come to, for here they were systematically punished for minor infractions.

Lagerälteste Zeingut frequently repeated the warning, after the escape attempt by the Dutch Jews, that if any *haeftlinge* (captive) tried to escape, every tenth prisoner would be shot. This, it was soon realized, was not an idle threat.

Camp food was terrible. It was more sparse than in previous camps and also contained entities designed to poison them. In their situation, such thoughts could hardly be dismissed as the product of an overworked imagination. The soup they received was official-ly designated 'spinach' soup, for it was a greyish-greenish sub-stance. But there, all resemblance to either 'spinach' or 'soup' ended. It was found to contain debris of all types, particles of dried straw and grass, even broken glass and sand. This soup was reserved especially for Jews and Bolsheviks. There were no spoons, and only a tin bowl from which one supped like an animal. But any type of fussiness would be misplaced here! It was no good thinking of meals at home, and the splendid china dishes which had been handed down as a family heirloom. No, better not think at all. Refuse to exercise the, by now, feeble 'gray matter.' Just concentrate on how to 'organize' a little more soup or a bit more bread than the thirty-three *dekas* which was the official allocation, or, on whether, looking up at the sky, which seemed perpetually mud-colored, there would be rain, for that would signify another discomfort to add to the already endless list.

These were the preoccupations against which they battled, day after day, minute after minute. Even to continue to breathe in and out became a minor triumph. The dishing out of the soup repre-sented a perilous time, for Braun the cook was notoriously bad-tempered. He would customarily lash out with either the soup ladle or any other implement at hand. A babble of sounds would emerge from the assembled mass. Polish Jews would cry out, "Oy vey …" Hungarian Jews, "Yoy, yoy …"

"The situation must have seemed to you quite hopeless then."

"Yes, yes it did. But, perhaps fortunately, we were shifted from place to place. One hardly had time to adjust to one place and to think, 'This is the worst. I can't go on,' when one was relocated quite suddenly and without warning. Then one felt again a slight flicker of optimism, perhaps, just perhaps this place will be a little better. Sometimes, there were slight improvements, sometimes not. In this way one remained always in a state of flux, never quite settled into despondency."

After Gräditz – Reichenbach

Reichenbach was the next stop in this kingdom of *lagers* and sub-camps. Here, the *haeftlinge*, in a state of unfounded anticipation at having left Gräditz behind, found their hopes soon dashed. Their work now consisted of laying an extension to existing railway lines. The *meister* in charge of supervising this task was named Nüzzler. Before the lines could be laid, the terrain needed to be leveled. For this purpose, trucks which the prisoners had to fill with dug-up earth waited in readiness. During this savage digging, which had to be maintained at a furious pace, prisoners daily dropped like flies. It was while engaged in this work, too, that Shmuel Reifer sustained his first serious injury. His foot somehow became entangled in the rail extensions as they began to lay them. As he tried in vain to extract the foot, he felt it becoming squeezed to the bone itself and knew that something of an irrevocable nature had been done to him. In excruciating pain, he was pulled free by his friends who then supported him back onto his feet. Somehow, the normally quick-witted kapo failed to notice him, and the boy completed his shift. Back in the barracks, an inmate with some knowledge of medical matters examined the now misshapen foot. Shrugging his shoulders, he turned to the boy who was pale with the effort of not allowing himself to cry out, "It is beyond repair. You will have to make do as best you can."

❧❧

Relocation from camp to camp usually took place secretly, in closed trucks, by night. Now followed a series of such unexplained moves. Their sojourn in Reichenbach lasted only a few weeks. Lying flat in the trucks, they were jolted and jerked as the vehicles moved rapidly over rough terrain. There was little time for queries or regrets. It was only at the moment of being thrust out of the trucks that they would turn to each other with questioning glances: "Is this a place for life or for death?"

Faulbrück and Markstedt

Faulbrück *lager* proved to be a camp in the league of Gräditz. Here, beatings and killings were the norm. The camp was positioned near the Zuckier factory, formerly owned by a Jew. Every morning the boy would walk two miles to work. His father and brother were in one column, with the Germans prodding them with their rifles: "Aufgehen, aufgehen." On this march they would customarily recite *Tehillim*. One Shabbos morning, as he was reciting the *Nishmas* prayer, the starving boy passed a German household. The lights were on and the family was gathered around the table, listening to the wireless radio. It was a normal, cozy family atmosphere. As Shmuel Reifer looked in on this scene, he happened to be reciting the words from the *Nishmas* prayer : *Ad heinah azarunu rachamecho, velo azavunu chasadecho, v'al titsheinu Hashem Elokeinu lanetzach — Up to this point Your mercy has helped us, and Your kindness has not forsaken us. Do not abandon us Hashem, our G-d, forever!*

At this point, as the boy pressed his nose against the window and gazed at the homey scene within, these words cut into the very fabric of his soul. Here they were, cut off from all normality, starved, lice-ridden, abandoned, lower than the lowest in G-d's kingdom. And he began to cry, tears of the gut, tears of the soul. His father turned to him: "Shmuel, my son, why do you cry?" But the tears continued to roll down his cheeks wordlessly, and he could give no answer.

Once again, this was to prove a temporary move. It was only when relocated to Markstedt some weeks later that the boy would emit a sigh of something akin to relief. Glancing around, with the eye of a *lager* veteran, he noticed that the place was cleaner and better organized than any camp he had as yet had the misfortune to inhabit. As dawn broke and the interminable *appel* was concluded, they were marched out to walk beneath the familiar sign crowning the camp's gate: '*Arbeit macht frei* — Work Makes You Free.' They were marched under a still darkened-sky through the icy fields to the accompaniment of jovial marching tunes played by the band of Jewish prisoners. These tunes transported them for a moment to another happier realm. Perhaps this was a festive band marching through quiet village streets. How the village children would clap and skip to the music! But what were they thinking of? No, here were no appreciative children to cheer them on, only the baying of the ever present SS dogs. Silhouetted against a harsh horizon in exact rows of five, only their feet moving left, right, left, right, this march of tired ghosts was nothing less than an outrageous parody and a deep offense against the music and the general goodwill of mankind.

> *The work itself was unbearable. This much they discovered after the first hour or two. It involved welding extensions to gas pipes, for the neighboring firm of Fg. Schlesien Ferngas. These pipes needed to be embedded deep within the soil. In winter, the ground was icy and unyielding, and digging the channels was not a simple matter. Some of the workers would*

stumble into the ditches. Needless to say, not infrequently it happened that they did not rise from there. Their work would begin at 7 in the morning and finish at 7 at night. During these twelve hours, they found themselves under the ever-vigilant eye of their meister who was, it soon became apparent, nothing less than a sadist. His stick was almost in constant use, and on the rare occasions when it was not, the meister twirled it incessantly. It was as if the stick was a 'thing' alive, itching to be in service, pitted mercilessly against a Jewish back. Of the five hundred slaves originally allocated for this pipe laying, less than one-fifth survived the long cruel winter.

Yitzchok Reifer

This winter was memorable for yet another reason. It was the season when 'Yitzchok' finally came into his own. Yitzchok was Shmuel's younger brother, and had been deported with him. Somehow, the trio — the two boys and their father — had managed to avoid separation, despite their constant change of location.

Yitzchok Reifer

Yitzchok was a remarkably adept young fellow, so it was not surprising that before too long he caught the eye of the SS. The SS supervisors were none too comfortable themselves that winter, for although they had the shelter of a small ramshackle shed in the area, they were nonetheless stranded in the middle of an out-of-the-way field. Retiring into this shed, they would leave the *haeftlinge* to their own supervisors, and to the *meister*, who had especially proved himself quite equal to the task.

The first errand on which the SS sent Yitzchok was to fetch drinking water for them. Fluent in German, he managed to ask directions to the nearest village, where he was directed toward a water pump. Thus he returned to the SS men, his mission successfully accomplished. On the next occasion, he was sent to a neighboring farm to see if he could procure some extra food. This time he was given some spare potatoes by a kindly village woman to take back to his SS men. Being unusually astute for his age, Yitzchok, who had virtually grown up with war and deprivation as his nursemaids, glimpsed a golden opportunity. He managed to obtain a few extra potatoes each time he was sent on an errand. These he would carry in his trousers and, as he passed his brother, he would let them drop.

"Quick, Shmuel, on the ground," he would whisper, as he passed. "Be sure to pass a potato or two on to father."

This welcome state of affairs lasted several months, with Yitzchok secure in his position as a favorite of the SS men.

When he heard their peremptory shout, "Schnell, komm aher," he knew immediately that it was he they wanted, for he had become more or less indispensable to them. Three or four times during the day this call would issue forth, and he would present himself promptly, ready to be of service. There were others in the miserable party of rain-sodden, half-frozen workers whom he managed to benefit with his 'potatoes.' One, Arcy Lipschitz, from his hometown Chrzanow, was in a particularly debilitated state. For those like Arcy, Yitzchok's potatoes represented life or death. As it transpired, these happenings did not go unnoticed for long. A kapo originally from Sosnowice was in charge of this squad of workers. Every day the sight of the fresh-faced boy, seemingly untouchable, moving with surety between the SS and the work lines, irritated him. The boy's cheerful grin led the Kapo to believe that he was up to something, and the Kapo was determined to find out exactly what that something was. "No one," he boasted to himself silently, "can get past me." The SS? Well, they were a different matter, he reflected, as the sounds of their half-drunken carousing reached his ears. He wrapped the winter coat, which he had special permission to don, firmly around him.

It was quite a simple matter to discover the offending potatoes and their source, so one morning this kapo with the pinched, sallow features, summoned Yitzchok.

"Now, listen here," he said, addressing the boy. "I know just what you're up to, you little shrimp. If you don't stop this potato smuggling, I'll report you to the SS. You won't be such an important 'macher' then!"

Yitzchok, however, was not unduly disturbed, for he did not seriously believe that even this warped individual would betray a fellow Jew to the SS. There were certain guidelines of behavior, even in the brutal universe which they now inhabited, that were rarely breached.

"Get back to work," the kapo cried, seeing the boy's smug expression. And at this he lashed out with his stick, caught in a sudden blind spasm of fury.

However, there is no knowing the human psyche. That evening, he made an official complaint in the camp, that the SS were being altogether too slack, and that as a result this particular work contingent was not being supervised well-enough. The matter was investigated and the guard was duly changed. The day that this occurred, Yitzchok's life-saving usefulness waned. It seemed that he had had 'his day,' and now the potatoes, as well as the other benefits, stopped.

⟡⟡

"Do you know that there is a postscript to this story?"
"Tell me how it happened."
"Well, many years later, I was walking on a New York street. You know how it is when you are confronted by a sea of faces, and suddenly you see a face from the past. For a moment or two you falter, for you cannot quite place the features. But you know the face, of that you are certain. Then enlightenment

dawns. Well, this happened to me, and when I finally placed the pinched, sallow features, I knew it to be none other than that particular kapo. In truth, he had changed little over the intervening years. But he now recognized me, it seemed, for he rushed forward, arm outstretched in a gesture of warm greeting.

"'Shmuel ... Shmuel Reifer ... Markstedt 19 ... Well, well, how are you?'

"'Go away,' I responded furiously.

"At this the fellow blanched visibly.

"'Do you think that either I or Yitzchok, or any of the others have forgotten what you did with the potatoes?'

"'It was different down there,' he interposed. 'I too was afraid for my life ... Everything was so different ... Come now, forgive and forget.'

"'Never,' I shouted at the top of my voice. 'I could never even bring myself to touch the tip of your fingers ... You are a betrayer of Israel.'

"By now, this betrayer realized that I was in deadly earnest. He mumbled something under his breath, 'be moichel me (forgive me),' and then beat a shamefaced retreat. Within seconds, he had melted back into the New York crowds and was indistinguishable. I stood for a long moment looking at the space into which he had vanished, and as it does from time to time, it seemed that the past threatened to overwhelm me, for it is all still here — do you know that? Do you understand that? It hasn't disappeared, no, not at all. Not a single scream or a tear, or a dying gasp ... It is all still here ... it's just that most of the time we don't see the pale army of the dead at our side."

On March 25th, 1944, *Rosh Chodesh Nissan*, a selection took place in the camp. It was snowing, but the inmates were told to remove all their clothing. Under an unpitying Polish sky, they were ordered to run past an improvised medical commission. The boy saw the desk with the stern-faced, bespectacled officials fingering their paperwork, then he broke into a slow trot. He tried to breathe in, in order to expand his rib cage and make him look a little fatter than he was. The damaged foot he dragged ever so lightly. As his pace quickened and he dipped his head as he finally passed the desk, he knew that he was running for his life. No childish races ever run in the Chrzanow streets against his friends from his block ever equaled this race for the right to draw breath. Panting, he stood in a group with the other two-legged 'animals,' thoroughly winded, demoralized, uncertain as to their futures. The megaphoned instructions continued to ring out all over Markstedt. By nightfall, the results of their 'running' had become apparent. The youth's number was called. He was destined, it seemed, to leave Markstedt, one of a group numbering one thousand *haeftlinge*. But he quickly realized that his father, with whom he had managed to remain all along, had not been selected. As the last of the sun's rays set on the filthy collection of barracks, he made his way to his father's hut.

"Father, I have been selected," he is close to tears. "We are moving out tonight … They say we are being moved to a new camp called Fünfteichen. But how can Yitzchok and I leave you here all alone?" And at this, Shmuel Reifer's voice finally breaks with the roughness of tears. And it is so long since he cried that he cannot for a moment understand what it is rolling down his cheeks in an unchecked flow.

"You must go, but wherever you go, promise me that you will look after Yitzchok for me," his father replies. "As for me, I will be fine. You see, I know the ins and outs here, and will really be quite comfortable." Here he attempts a sardonic smile, but the sight of the boy's tears stops him.

The boy sees something else. He sees how hollow and emaciated his father's cheeks have grown, how weary he looks, how defeated. And in that instant he thinks, prophet-like, "I will never see him again."

Another member of the selected group rushes in.

"Shmuel, you must come now. We are leaving."

"Father, bless me," the boy says.

So, the father places his thin hands on the lad's head and pronounces the ancient words.

"May the L-rd bless you and safeguard you. May the L-rd light up His countenance for you, and be gracious to you. May the L-rd turn His countenance to you and grant you peace." And at the word 'peace (shalom),' Shmuel is gone.

After leaving their father, the two brothers were marched onto the train. But they were dejected and apathetic. Did it matter where they were being taken? Father, whom they had both struggled to protect, was left behind. They were no longer a family, but two young boys cut adrift in a faceless sea of humanity.

Leaning his head against the train wall, at that moment Shmuel Reifer thought: "It is enough. So, they have won after all … I give in … Let me die here. I no longer agree to be shunted here and there like cattle. Let the end come."

But Yitzchok was pulling at his sleeve. He seemed frightened and vulnerable, no longer recognizable as the erstwhile darling of the SS.

"But I have a brother," he thinks, "and father charged me to look after him … I must pull myself together."

Fünfteichen – Berta Work Krupp

The camp, when they arrived, looked so similar to Markstedt that they actually may have entertained the fanciful notion that they had been put on a train and taken back to where they had started.

However, they soon discovered that there were differences. For one thing, this was a much larger camp, containing internees from many nationalities. The non-Jewish prisoners were treated in a fairly humane way. They were not beaten or shot. They received regular parcels from home, letters and cigarettes. But the treatment meted out to the Jews was the very worst, worse by far than that reserved for murderers and criminals. It was here, too, in Fünfteichen, that there was a new change in their condition. They were finally made to don the striped pajamas which they had managed to avoid wearing in the other *lagers*. These pajamas did not have pockets, and the men were not provided with undergarments. Hygienic conditions were poor as usual. There was a communal bathroom which consisted of several buckets. These were for their use and they were each given two bars of soap. In this *lager* they were also tattooed with numbers. Shmuel's number was 25440.

At 5:30 a.m., they were marched out to work again in strict formations of five. Again the camp musicians 'serenaded' them in mock celebration of their condition. The work was as brutal and senseless as in the other camps. Massive hand-trucks were located on one side. These, they were given to understand, were to be filled with sacks of cement. The prisoners would then have to roll these trucks down the hill, empty them, and then begin the whole process again. What was the purpose of this sisyphus-like work? Its underlying uselessness haunted them. No, there was no purpose for it other than to crush the breath out of their bodies and shatter their spirits. They knew it in their darker moments, trudging with the convoy. To add to their miseries, the cold wind lashed at them in their flimsy prison uniforms. But despair forced them to inventiveness and, whenever possible, they used the paper bags which had held the cement to line their clothing and give them a little extra protection.

After work, shivering and exhausted, they were not yet allowed to retire, for here, the infamous German sense of humor came into play. They were not 'fit' enough, it had been decided, and would benefit from some muscle stretching and toning.

To this end, they were forced to balance glass bottles while mounting and dismounting from wooden stools, to do pushups on beds of stones, stand on one leg and touch the ground. The inventiveness of their tormentors seemed bottomless. Their amusement at a group of half-dead *haeftlinge* struggling through their paces, knew no bounds.

In those moments, lifting their heads from their squatting position to see first a shiny boot, next a thick truncheon, and finally, the corners of a Germanic mouth spread upwards in uncurtailed merriment, the prisoners were consumed by a deep and burning hatred.

"One day — one day soon — we will get even."

But most of the time these moments were as rare as a flower sprouting in the slow-moving mud. For Shmuel Reifer, in common with his co-sufferers, felt very little.

"I worry about father. Do you think he is managing without us to organize those little extras for him?"

"Don't worry. He himself told us he would be fine."

"How long before we will be united back in Chrzanow. Mother and the girls must be concerned what has happened to us."

"It will not be much longer, I am sure. There is so much talk of things going against them now." (Does he suppress the unconscious irony which he feels underlies this 'simple' conversation? Yitzchok is an unusually intelligent youngster. He must see what is happening around them as something larger and more pervasive.)

"Shmuel, I want to go home. When will it all end?"

"Soon, very soon. And we will go back there together. This much I promise you."

"Did you seriously believe the promises you gave Uncle Yitzchok?"

"Oh, but that is a question which is not a question, in my opinion. We spoke very little in those days, for even communication had become a luxury to us. When you have just pushed a truck loaded with cement up and down, all day long, believe me, you have very little desire to engage in conversation. Mostly, we retreated into ourselves and into our

> *own private struggle to stay alive. And when we did talk, it*
> *was in the manner of Bilaam's donkey; we opened our mouths*
> *and somehow, miraculously, the words came out. But our*
> *words were not connected with our thoughts, for our thoughts*
> *were different. I dreamed of Chrzanow and home, and thought*
> *'where are mother and the girls right now?' But it was like a*
> *thing remote, belonging to a dream. It was not so much that*
> *we suspected that they did not exist any longer, but that we*
> *did not see how we could ever, in our terribly weakened*
> *conditions, get back there. 'Take me there, take me back,' our*
> *spirits would murmur, but our emaciated bodies would give*
> *their own answer."*

≈≈

Gerlitz – Shmuel Reifer's Final Camp

As soon as Shmuel Reifer had become accustomed to one set of conditions, he would once more be on the move. It was as if the Third Reich itself had conspired against him: "You shall have no rest. You shall wander the face of our dreadful kingdom." So, after a few months' sojourn in a particular *lager*, or as soon as he had come to know the barracks, the SS men, the kapos, the peculiar conditions of work, the specific way the sun set over the high voltage wires and the fences, which allowed you to see outside but not to be seen, in the back of his mind, the thought grew: "Soon I shall be moved." It was July 1944. They knew the date vaguely from fragments of information that reached them regularly from the 'vast outside.' It was a beautiful summer's day, and Shmuel, in an uncharacteristic aside, remarked to Yitzchok, "Well, it's perfect picnic weather. What do you say we pack a basket and go off somewhere? You choose the spot. "And then, out of the corner of his eye, he saw the bustle of arrivals. This was taking place towards the entrance of the camp. Shmuel turned to his fellow inmate and casually asked, "What's going on? Who are the lucky fish?"

"It's the fellows from the Warsaw Ghetto, the ones they flushed out like rats, from the ruins. Yeshik told me about them."

At this, they lapsed into silence, for they had heard of those who had resisted the German army. Every day had brought fresh news of them. Now, looking as defeated spiritually as the rest of them, they were here.

The next day, yet another consequence of this amazing happening was to transpire. The Warsaw boys, despite their prolonged struggle, were in better physical shape than many of the *lager* inmates. Besides that, room would have to be made to accommodate them. In short, there was to be a selection. It was Monday morning when Shmuel Reifer and the others were finally marched out of Fünfteichen, and marched onto the trains. Their belts and shoes were taken away from them, and they were loaded into three carriages. The trains moved, and they were on their way again, shunted like the sacks of cement they had transported, across the Polish countryside. As they climbed into the trains, there had been one or two wisecracks: "Shall we choose the first-class or the second class carriage?" "Oh, the ticket collector is neglecting us." But the jokes had ceased by the time the first night fell.

This was like a recurrent dream. Again, the cattle cars, the only light filtering in through a tiny wired opening, the stench, the lack of food or drink. This time it was very hot and the lack of water, in particular, tormented them. They felt the wagons steaming in the July sun, and inside the carriages their bodies rattled like dried peas in a pod. They were shriveling up now, drying out altogether. Soon, there would barely be enough left of them, only the brain which — remarkably — still registered fear. They would not be worth a bullet in the back. They could be snuffed out soundlessly, like candles, without even a final cry of anguish or revenge. And even their tears would come to nothing.

"*Ribbono Shel Olam,*" the boy thought, "let us be remembered … don't let us die here in the cattle cars."

As the third night fell, the train screeched to a halt. No one stirred. Next, the doors to the carriages were flung open to the usual accompanying shouts, and the barking of dogs. Still, no response. They were like an inert, entangled, steaming mass. Now the SS men grew agitated. "Raus, raus …," they screamed. They jumped up onto the carriages, treading on feet, hands, heads. They hacked away at the bodies until one was released, then another. The men then stood on their feet. They teetered. They began to walk. In this way, they made their entrance into Gerlitz. [3]

Gerlitz, Block 28

Their new abode was Gerlitz Block 28, their new address if you like. Their *lagerälteste*, who made the customary speech of introduction, was a German national called Czech who had murdered his wife. He was blind in one eye. As he spoke, he shifted from one foot to the other and fingered a wicked-looking lead pipe; its purpose left little to the imagination. He left the block, having initiated the new internees into the 'rules' at Gerlitz. The barracks was, in point of fact, a large, empty building so they lay on the floor. They were still shoeless, for in this state they had left Fünfteichen. They lay, a mass of bodies as in the carriages, hungry, weary, beyond thought or even fear. On what must have been the third day, they were called to *appel*. At *appel* they realized that Gerlitz comprised about ten thousand inmates.

After *appel*, they found that release was not yet at hand. There were a series of 'exercises' to be endured. First, there was 'drill' in cap removal. "Hats on, hats off." Then the exercises they had been subjected to in Fünfteichen, rolling around in the mud, chicken-style, rising up and down from a chair, balancing a bottle on one's head, crawling on all fours. Shmuel Reifer thought that these 'exer-

---

3. Yitzchok remained in Fünfteichen. He was reunited with his brother Shmuel only at the end of the war, after having been taken on a march to Buchenwald.

cises,' this 'drilling,' represented the ultimate blow to what remained of their humanity. One was at once a rolling ball, an automaton, rising, kneeling, crawling on command. And with no will of one's own, one was scarcely human. One was a zero, a nothing. One could be blown away too, disposed of, in just such disciplined fashion. Obey the command. Allow oneself to be done away with. It was painless enough when even the spirit no longer rose in rebellion.

The next day was still spent in initiation rites. First, they were 'hosed' down with huge rubber pipes. Next, came *entlausung*, the delousing process, using caustic chemicals. This took place at some point in the middle of the night. A 'louse promenade' was formed down the center of each head, for the ostensible reason of lice-prevention, but also branding them unmistakably as *haeftlinge*. In reality, the lice could not be controlled. Chemicals did not help, nor did the shaving. They penetrated beneath the skin and sucked the blood. They were worse than the hunger, for they ate up their victims from the inside.

In the barracks, they soon found conditions to be appalling. The roofs were leaking, and there was no form of heating for the winter. There was nothing to cover oneself with, no blankets of any description. The food, too, was worse than in other camps. It was of the same type, the coffee, the so-called 'spinach soup,' but less of it. But it was at Gerlitz that Shmuel Reifer was finally assigned indoor work, which represented a not-inconsiderable stroke of luck.

Accused of Sabotage

Situated near the Gerlitz *lager*, which was in a small town, (the railway was used both by the *lager* and the town), was a factory called 'Wagonen Maschinen Bau.' Accordingly, the *meisters* from this factory would periodically visit the *lager* to take their pick of the slave labor. At one of these selections Shmuel Reifer was chosen as one of a group of a hundred, and one summer's morning was duly marched out of the *lager* gates toward a low, sprawling building. He was glad, he thought, remembering the horrific pipe track laying of the previous winter. His only cause for regret was that 12-year-old Yitzchok had not been chosen along with him.

Work at the factory began at 6 a.m. and ended at 6 in the evening. The Jewish prisoners arriving on their first day felt as awkward as children at their first day of school. They arrived in the wooden shoes which had now been handed out, and as they shifted noisily onto the highly polished factory floor, all eyes were turned towards them. For the first time in months, they experienced a sense of shame at their disheveled and dehumanized condition for, momentarily, they saw themselves through the eyes of those inhabiting the 'normal' world. The painfulness of this realization burned through them like searing irons.

The factory had several bathrooms for the workers' use, and for the first few weeks, they were allowed to use them. It seemed to them, in those moments, that they had fallen into paradise. But, the spell was soon broken. The mistake was discovered and an edict issued. The bathrooms were strictly out of bounds to Jewish workers. Other privileges, too, were denied to them. If a factory worker proved himself diligent, he could earn extra bread and even cigarettes. In their case, however, these were confiscated by the *lagerälteste* as soon as they returned to the camp at night. This group incurred the wrath and jealousy of the *blockälteste* too, and the boy was not infrequently beaten quite mercilessly on his return to his barracks.

It was while employed in the factory that the youth was caught in a so-called 'act of sabotage.' Employed on the factory floor, his job was drilling holes in metal parts for tanks. One day, a pile of hinges was found on a neighboring table by a German officer, *Meister* Muller. These hinges were found, on examination, to have the holes drilled in the wrong places. "These hinges have been missing, now they turn up next to yours. Furthermore, some of the hinges have deliberately been tampered with. I tell you what I think, I think that you know something of this matter," he said, drawing out the last word deliberately.

He clicked his feet and turned on his heel.

Five minutes later, he returned with a superior, who cut the electricity to the boy's machine with one swift movement.

Meister Muller indicated the pile. His superior, peering shortsightedly through his glasses, nodded:

"Yes," he said at last, "I agree with you, *Meister* Muller. You were right to call me. There is something more going on. Furthermore, by these actions ...," and he nodded in the direction of the quaking boy, "the prestige of Germany is being lowered in the eyes of other nations," he added in the clipped, precise tones of party-propaganda. And with a surreptitious glance, he indicated the other nationals hard at work on the factory floor.

At that moment, the boy was engaged in looking beyond the SS men, towards the window, and noticing a single perfectly formed snowflake languidly drift across it, as if time was of no importance. "Am I of less importance than that snowflake?" he wondered. "Is my existence more tenuous? Have I survived until now," he thought, "to be beaten to death in some dark, nameless cellar?" And then the thought simultaneously occurred to him: "And what of my father? How will he survive without me?"

But there was no more time to think. He was frog-marched off by the two men. They strutted self-importantly ahead of him, for they had discovered no less than a 'grand subterfuge.' Again, the accusation was leveled at the boy in front of the kapo. The malproduced hinges were found not far from the boy's seat. As this work was vital for the war effort, the conclusion that must be drawn is that the youth either masterminded an act of sabotage, or was assisting others to this end. They simultaneously turned towards the boy:

"Kindly disclose who has set you up to this and you will be free to go back to your work."

The boy shook his head.

"What do you mean? Speak up, speak up."

"It has nothing to do with me and I know nothing about it. I can tell you nothing."

"Nothing, nothing? Eh … eh …?"

"Let's send you to Gross Rosen. There they will think it a 'hanging matter.'

At this the *lagerälteste, Czech,* spoke up.

"No, no, don't hang the boy. Give him a stiff punishment, say fifty lashes."[4]

At this, *Meister* Muller produced a thick stick. The boy's head was forced down between his legs and the beating commenced. Perhaps fifty, sixty blows rained down on him in steady succession. He had stopped counting. A tremendous crack. The stick has broken. With a curse, *Meister* Muller called for a rubber truncheon. The blows began again. Blood spurted under the renewed assault, but the boy had shut his mind off. The pain could not reach him, and he felt instinctively that Muller was wearing himself out to no purpose.

"Tell, tell, I beg you," Muller screamed. He was now at the mercy of the youth, for only his 'telling' could release him from this cycle of bloody blow-dealing. Muller's arm was tired. Sweat dripped from his forehead, he longed for release, if possible, more than his victim.

But the boy had nothing to tell. He was back in Chrzanow, reliving that quiet night when Grandfather Reifer was dragged half-dead over their threshold. He had won by silence too. He, too, had nothing to confess. And, at any rate, had he known any names, he would never have divulged them. Silence — the silence that is beyond words, beyond cries or blows, beyond suffering … the silence that flies like a skylark up to the Heavenly throne itself, and there, finally, speaks its message — that is the silence which he now espoused.

But Muller has stopped. He is spluttering.

"Take him away — out of my sight, *stünk* Jude. He is done for."

---

4. It was a miracle that Czech a German criminal who had murdered his wife, spoke up in this manner. In fact, in so doing, he saved the boy's life.

Then he collapsed into a wooden chair, mopping his brow with a large white handkerchief. "These Jews ..." he continued to mutter and curse under his breath.

Shmuel Reifer was dragged down to an airless cellar, and left for dead. How many days he lay there motionless he would never know. Finally, he felt a hand on his collar. The hand was firm — it yanked him to his feet and then pulled him after it into daylight. The boy stood blinking at the grayish winter light. It was Hirsch Spalter.

"I am taking you back," he said.

"Back where?"

"To your machine, of course. You've had a nice vacation, which is more than others can boast of."

Lying in a bloody heap next to his machine where Hirsch Spalter had deposited him, for all the world like a packet of misdirected mail, he could not even raise his head, and might never raise it again. Voices rose and fell about him, and there was a steady hum of machinery. Then he heard a familiar shuffling of feet, and then silence.

"What goes on here?" a harsh SS voice. "Why has this prisoner not gone for his soup?"

He took a closer look at the boy, taking in his general condition.

"Call the kapo. He has been beaten up. We will get to the bottom of this suspicious matter!"

The kapo was sent for. He arrived thoroughly alarmed.

"Who is responsible for this? Who has beaten this Jew? Don't you realize that we have all nationalities working on this factory floor and this will simply not do. How will it look?" he appealed to the kapo. The kapo obviously was a Jew and knew that all over Poland they were burning Jews by the cattle-car load, and no one was concerned how it 'may look.' But in this case, a public display of violence, which may be noted by other nationals, would simply not 'do'!

"Sir," he offered tentatively. "I think I know who is responsible."

All this time, while his 'case' is under discussion, Reifer lies slumped across a wooden-backed chair. He could not control his head movements, tried hard to focus, but succeeded only in drooping forward again onto his chest.

Several minutes elapsed. The factory door opened and shut — there was the sound of feet running.

Muller finally rushed in, his face aflame like a beetroot.

"Are you responsible for this — this —" and the SS man searched for an appropriate word, "this debacle?" he brings out at last.

"But sir," Muller began, "you do not understand. This is a clear case of sabotage. You see —"

"Silence," roared his superior.

"Do you know how much this sort of thing does to endanger our image? I will speak to your immediate supervisor. This is an outrage," and he turned smartly on his heels.

Muller, left alone with his victim, surveyed the crumpled, blood-stained heap.

"*Vast hast du gemacht?*" he brought out finally in a voice thick with hate. He offered a lame imitation of a kick, "*Weck mit dem schwein,*" and simultaneously grabbed hold of the boy's collar. For the second time, that day, he was yanked unceremoniously to his feet. He found himself hauled firmly out of the factory doors. They walked silently side by side, tormentor and victim. At last, they reached the camp and he was thrust back through the gates into the 'life' of the *lager*.

Muller stood watching him, hands on hips, until the boy was finally indistinguishable from the other pajama-clad prisoners, inmates of the *lager* known as Gerlitz. Only then did he let out a sigh, as he turns back towards the relative security of his small office.[5]

> "How did you manage after this beating?"
> "Well, in point of fact, I was by now in very poor
> condition. I was emaciated from hunger and my lungs were

---

5. *Meister* Muller was ultimately sent to Siberia.

weak. The injury I had received on the rail tracks had never totally healed, and this beating was the final blow. Some of these scars I still have. At that time, most of my fellow prisoners did not expect me to survive. I was described as 'being finished, done for — kaput.' And to all intents and purposes, I was. But who can define the logistics of survival? Some who seemed fittest among us survived only to die of overeating, or typhoid, days after liberation, while others, like myself, who were in such poor condition, outlived them. 'The secret things belong to the L-rd' – this is what we say, and what we believe. There is so much about what happened 'down there' that we will never truly understand."

Freedom Dawns

In the Gerlitz *lager*, ostensibly cut off from the world, news from the 'outside' nevertheless began to permeate the prison walls, drip by steady drip.

Now that Germany was losing the war the prisoners experienced a sudden surge of interest which they had not felt for all these dead months or years. In this hellish kingdom, which had been constructed especially for their benefit, cracks were beginning to appear. Heads down they had slept, ate, worked in the required manner. Only at very infrequent intervals, punctuating the darkness, had there come a spark of inspiration, by which some of them understood that the system which was, to all intents and purposes, impregnable, and would last forever and ever until there was no longer a species called 'Jew' on the face of the earth, might possibly be outlived. They would, with much peril, light a Chanukah candle in one corner of their miserable barracks, or murmer the words of the Purim *Megillah*. Then they would recall that every Pharaoh and every Haman has his brief 'day' but eventually wanes into nothingness. But the Jew always lives on. What of the piles of bodies they had all heard spoken of, the daily killings, the stranglings and shootings? They would never *all* be killed. Logic and history told them this. Jews would die, many Jews, but the generic Jew would remain. A remnant would survive, and not only survive, but live to tell the story.

What they had all noticed in the manner of the SS men of late, but which they had not openly discussed among themselves, was a new furtiveness of manner. Where they had once been so cocksure, now there crept into their tone a sense of questioning. They actually met the eyes of the prisoners now, as if they were asking the questions, "How much longer will you be prisoners and we your masters? Perhaps, this whole world will be stood on its head, and we will soon have to beg mercy from you." This is what their glances seemed to portend. When they looked at a *haeftlinge* now, it was with a new eye that saw beyond the striped-pajama-clad, miserable, shivering creature, fodder to the daily death machine, to a new era, ruled by very different contingencies. The SS man's gaze would falter, a look almost of self-pity flitting over his features.

This was what the *haeftlinge* observed in those uneasy days leading up to spring. The persistent rumors and eventually the sound of guns, as the front drew closer, created an impression of some terrible unknown end, some veritable doomsday being close at hand.

Shmuel Reifer was, to all intents and purposes, a dead man when the first cracks appeared in the nightmarish edifice. Rife with infections, he was, in fact, little more than a skeleton, weighing sixty pounds in all. As he flitted in and out of consciousness on his filthy straw palette, he knew that something of earth-shattering proportions was transpiring. "Hang on, hang on," an inner voice seemed to say. "But I have no strength, I am done for," another voice argued back. "Let me go the way of all the others, one more dead Jew in Europe." He would have liked to see the Chrzanow of his youth just one more time, but he knew instinctively that that was gone, gone irrevocably. Someone was whispering words in his ear: "Shmuel, it is Shabbos, Shabbos in the *lager*!" and immediately, letting his head drop back on the straw, he was back in Chrzanow. His mother had covered her head with a white kerchief and was blessing the candles. All the tension of the arduous preparations had drained from her as she prayed with every fiber of her small frame for the well-being of her husband and children. There was a moment of utter peace and serenity, and he remembered, as a child, wishing to hold on to that moment. A shadow hovered over him. It was his neighbor from the bunk above him.

Zittau

February 5th, 1945. The Russian army was now nearing and the Germans were desperate to conceal the horror which was Auschwitz. Even in the death throes of the Third Reich, the German killing machine was still active. Prisoners were taken on a march from various concentration camps to Zittau, further to the west.

One of the boy's most horrific war memories was that the SS appeared twice daily to count how many *verstünkene Juden* were still alive, and how many had died. One day the SS man recognized the youth Reifer. His reaction was immediate. He clenched his fist at him, as he spotted him still alive amongst the pile of 'Jew-garbage,' shouting on top of his voice, "*Das schwein Jude lebt noch* — The Jew dog is still alive?!*"

At the same camp there was a well-known artist from Paris called Jonnie Glucksman, who had contracted typhoid. Since the doctor had not disclosed this to the SS, Glucksman ended up lying next to the youth. As he was a well-known personality, he was given bread and soup but he could barely eat, as he was too weak.

The youth, in his famished condition, finished the food Glucksman had left, yet by some miracle of miracles he did not contract the dreaded typhoid.

It was on a Tuesday that liberation finally came. The Shabbos before, the boy fell asleep so weak and desperate that he had lost all hope of surviving. That night he dreamt that he appeared before the *Beis Din Shel Ma'alah* — the Heavenly Court above — and he was standing in front of the Judge of all humanity.

Suddenly, he saw an old man named Shimon Moishe Groner, who would regularly come to his yeshivah to say *Tehillim* and to learn. The *Beis Din Shel Ma'alah* ordained that because Shmuel had learned *behasmadah gedolah,* with fervent concentration, he would be given added years of life.

In the morning he awoke with a strange sensation. Although he was still extremely weak, he suddenly felt that there was hope.

Evacuation of the Camp

Two days later, the Germans began to evacuate the camp. Gradually, every nook and cranny was vacated by them, the watchtowers, the control offices, the sleeping quarters. Now they were leaving the 'cities,' which they had built specifically to destroy Jews and other undesirables, to whoever was still left alive. The stench of death lay thickly in the air. This they could not conceal, although they tried desperately to remove incriminating documents. That this place, and all the others, had been death camps would soon be discovered by the world.

At this point, the 'living dead' were told: "You are free. You may leave the camp." However, this necessitated rising on one's two feet and walking out. This was not so easily accomplished. Shmuel Reifer, being one of those unable to walk, simply stayed behind. At this point, beyond all earthly cares, he awaited his fate.

≈❦≈

Prisoners began to leave in slow trickles. It was difficult to grasp the concept that they were free, that they could go where they wished. A fellow called Rosmarin, who had been lying in the next bunk to Reifer, stood up on his feet. For a moment or two he tottered uncertainly, like an infant about to take his first steps, then he walked away. A few hours later he returned. He was now wearing a suit, which hung on him tent-like. And most unbelievably of all, he was carrying an enormous bowl of noodles. The 'living dead' now questioned him.

"Where did you get this?"

"Well," he replied. "It happened like this. I walked into Zittau itself and hammered on the first door I came to. A German woman opened the door. She stared at me, terrified.

"'Will you leave us alive?' she pleaded.

"'All right,' I said.

"'Well, you may come in,' she said.

She showed me to the bathroom. Then she gave me a haircut and fitted me out with underwear. Next she gave me food to eat. Finally, she filled this huge bowl with *lokshen*." Rosmarin, mad with joy, put his finger into the *lokshen* and began throwing it everywhere.

May 9th 1945 – Freedom

On this date, freedom became not just a word to bandy about, but a fact. A Red Army patrol drove into the camp. The Russians had arrived. They knew themselves to be witnesses to some all-pervading evil. All over Europe the Allies were making similar discoveries, and these discoveries would change humanity's view of itself forever.

Slightly disorientated, the Russians inhaled the death stench. They began to investigate the barracks. Slowly, singly, like survivors of a world gone mad, the victims were beginning to emerge from the smoking ruins.

The first to reach Shmuel Reifer was Captain Vasser, from Kiev. He grasped the boy's thin shoulders in a bear-like hug. The boy was skeletal and gasped in pain, but still the captain would not let go of his shoulder.

Hot tears flowed down Captain Vasser's cheeks: "I am a Jew, Vasser from Kiev. What have they done to you? What have they done?!"

In this manner, Shmuel Reifer from Chrzanow, inmate of eight concentration camps, was finally liberated.

❦❦

By May 10th, the boy was in a Zittau hospital near Dresden. For weeks he was extremely ill, hovering between life and death, passing in and out of consciousness, like a night train speeding through lit-up stations, not stopping. He dreamed. He was in a cell and he was being beaten methodically, around the head and back.

"Tell us all you know," *Meister* Muller's red-hued face hangs over him like an overripe beetroot.

"I know nothing. Nothing. Leave me alone."

He dreamed again. He is walking with his father. They walk and walk endlessly. But he has his hand in his father's pocket. This the SS somehow do not notice. Their fingertips are touching. But Father's fingers are so cold, so cold. He, Shmuel, must warm them. All of a sudden Father is ordered on ahead. He tries to keep pace with him, but somehow, his feet will not carry him faster. And Father is floating, or perhaps flying on ahead. He is moving so quickly that already he is out of reach. He is striding forward into the gray, uncertain mist.

The boy awakens for a moment. Shadows pass over his bed. There is whiteness here and also something flowered. He is bewildered, he cannot make it out. Surely there are no flowers in the *lager* …

He is back in his dream. He is on his own street, about to knock on his own front door. His sister answers. Mother and Father are sitting around the Shabbos table. They are talking gaily together and passing around fragrant dishes. The fragrance assails his nostrils. He opens his mouth to speak. "It is I, Shmuel. I have come back." But strangely, they all ignore him. "Oh, I have been through so much. Only give me a little time and I will tell you all." They continue chatting, but look up from time to time, as if they sense the presence of another.

"Mother, Father, I am back, I am back. Speak to me," he screams out.

The tears roll down his sunken cheeks as they turn from him.

"I want to tell my story, but no one will listen."

By October, the boy was out of bed and could manage a few steps, aided by a stick, but his lungs were still weak, and he continued to undergo frequent X-rays. It was established that he had tuberculosis of the right lung. There was very little to eat in the hospital, but it was much more than he had had in the camps. He was, however, tormented by a terrible hunger, which was more psychological than physiological. He would frequently wake up in the middle of the night to eat, as though he feared that if he waited until the morning, the food would no longer be there. During these months, his father's cousin, Chazkel Reifer, also an inmate in the hospital, was a frequent visitor, as was his rescuer Captain Vasser. The most frequent subject of their discussions was not the past, but the future. What should he do now? Where to go? The boy had one longing fixed in his heart — to return to his hometown. The cousin argued against it. The possibility of finding anyone alive there was remote and the youth was in no condition to travel. Although the boy probably admitted to the objective truth of these statements, in his heart he remained adamant.

He would be detained no longer. If he could reach Chrzanow, the whole of the frightful nightmare of the past few years would be blotted out, and life would simply resume its peaceful ways. He would enter the family business and take over the timber yard. Everything would become simple and easy to understand again. One autumn day, therefore, he simply dismissed himself from the hospital, hav-

My father's cousin, Chazkel Reifer, 1946

ing procured a letter from the hospital administration saying that he was from the camps. (He also had a stamped letter from Major Vasser confirming his identity and the nature of his complaint.)

"Did you know deep down that it was a delusion?"

"Yes, of that there is no doubt. It was like a mirage in the desert towards which you journey, knowing that when you get to it, it will simply fade into nothingness. But you delude yourself. In reality, this is how you continue living; we all do this in lesser ways. But we had survived a terrible cataclysm, something unthinkable. There were simply no resources for dealing with this. What happened to me immediately after the liberation is part of the story too. Perhaps, to this very day, we are still 'living the story.' I simply do not know."

Going home proved to be no easy task. This became apparent as soon as he had taken his first steps outside the hospital's environs. Where should he go? In which direction? Zittau was near Dresden. However, on reaching the station it soon became apparent that there were no trains. Zittau was not far from the Polish border, but apparently the only way to reach Poland was on a train leaving from Koblenz. From there one could board a Russian military train. This the boy eventually managed to do, against all odds. It was a freezing October night. Finding a place on top of an open goods train, surrounded by rough-speaking Russian soldiers, bitter thoughts haunted him. "Is this what I was liberated for?"

"Who is this?" a Russian soldier shone a lamp directly in his face.

"This boy is from the camps," the Russian reiterated in wonder, as if surprised to see such a specimen.

"When does the train start?" the boy asked naively.

Raucous laughter broke out around him.

"Well, let us see," the Russian bellowed. "It could be half an hour and it could be a week."

His comrades subsided into helpless laughter.

"See here, a Russian train has a mind of its own — like everything else Russian!" he concluded, slapping his knee.

Deciding there was little hope of this 'Russian' train ever taking him anywhere, the boy alighted but not before his watch and his precious ration of bread were taken from him. This the Russian gave to his German fiance. It was at this point that the boy felt that he had reached his lowest ebb. Had he survived all the horrors of the war only to be victimized again? Not possessing the strength to walk away, he lay down on the floor and proceeded to shed bitter tears. After a while, he managed to lift himself and make his way to the office of the Russian High Command. In a voice that cracked with anger he explained how a Russian soldier had stolen his few possessions and he demanded justice. The soldier was summoned and identified, and the watch recovered, but not the bread.

Within days he found himself back in the town of Gerlitz, just a few kilometers from where he had been incarcerated. By such fits and starts the boy's progress was measured. From Gerlitz, he found himself on a military transport taking survivors of the camps back to Poland. A day later, he was in Cracow. But it was not the Cracow he remembered. The vibrant Jewish life, six centuries old, was to all intents and purposes gone. A sickening fear tore at his innards, more desolate than any he had known since he had been liberated from Gerlitz. Perhaps his cousin had been right and there was simply nothing to come back to. Dare he go to Chrzanow? No, no he argued with himself, in Chrzanow it would be different!

The following day he left for home. Never had the boy felt so alone. And what was he seeking? He was seeking to reestablish the old reality. Was that so much to ask? He arranged to be let off by the taxi a few streets away from the Jewish quarter, for he wanted to walk the rest of the way. The streets began to look familiar. Like a bell tolling, his heart throbbed in measured spasms. And it seemed to him that he was seeing all this, but with altered eyes. People passed him on the street — some looked vaguely familiar — but no Jews. One or two stood and stared at him as if seeing something unexpected. Now he was on his own street. Superficially, the buildings looked the same, unscarred by the terrible years. The tree at the corner was still there, the lamppost, every paving stone. He was mentally ticking off trivial items on a list: "This is the same, that is the same," as if steeling himself against that fathomless void, which all that time, in his heart of hearts, he knew to be curled at the bottom like a snake.

"See, see your fears are groundless? It is all the same. What nonsense! How could this ever change? It is like a rock — immortal, immune, unalterable ..."

He reached the apartment building itself and entered the hallway. His hand reached up to the bell.

"Let the moment come," he prays, "quick, quick ..."

A surly Pole half opens the door.

"What do you want?"

A mistake. "I live here!"

"Speak up, boy. What is it you say?!"

A misunderstanding. But he is back in his dream, the one in which he returns home to tell his story and is ignored. "I am real," something in him cries. "Not insubstantial as air, not a mere *luftmensch*. I will not be blown away."

"I come from the camps. We used to live here!"

"Ah, so that's it. You are a Jew, a Yid!" a slow gleam of understanding dawns in the Pole's eye. "So how come," he says with a cunning intonation, "you are still alive? I thought Hitler took care of you all!"

This last argument is unanswerable.

"Anyway," the Pole concluded, growing impatient. "I have no time to stand all day in idle talk. We have been living here for the past three years. What is it you want here?"

"It's nothing, nothing at all," the boy mutters, more to himself. "I was only looking for my past ..."

"So that is the end of the story?"

"Yes, I suppose so. I had come full circle. Of course, as I have said, one could go on, for there are no truly clear definitions of where it begins and where it ends.

"After that, I wandered aimlessly for a while, like an autumn leaf blown in the wind. I suppose I went back to Cracow, for that was the nearest town, and there were a handful of Jews there who had organized themselves a little. They had formed a Jewish Committee dealing with the needs of Holocaust survivors. Also, I heard that an uncle of mine was in Cracow. I finally found him, renting drafty rooms on the third floor of a large block of flats overlooking the Vistula. Somehow, at this point I must have lapsed into my old illness again and was admitted to the Krankestube on Luga 38. Here, I remained for a period of weeks, months even. I remember my uncle and aunt Jeret, who had aged over the past few years, being regular visitors and bringing me food. (Another visitor was Stern, Schindler's accountant, who outlined the major part played by my uncle Jeret in the Schindler interlude.) I was treated by a Dr. Lew (a surviving Schindler Jew who gave me preferential treatment because of his respect for my uncle). It was a light, a faint whiff of home, having them there at that time. It was like the scent of rain on a summer's day, something inherently remote yet consoling. So I recovered, gradually, but was never really well for about two years. In between, I found work in a small timber factory."

"So you stayed on in Poland. What made you leave eventually?"

"Well, there came, as there so often does, a turning point. For me, in an emotional sense, it was the pogrom that occurred in Kielce on June 4th, 1946. Things were far from easy for Jewish survivors at that time. They had come back from the camps or from Russia with literally nothing but the clothes they stood in. Poland was a cemetery, a river of Jewish blood. They had lost their families, homes, businesses, everything. But they had gravitated back, because they did not know what else to do. It was a habit of mind, an instinct that drove them back to our old breeding ground. In Kielce, some seventy to eighty Jews were living in a community house in great poverty. One day, a middle-aged Polish woman announced that her son was missing. She claimed that the Jews had abducted him to make their matzos for Pesach. It was the blood-libel of the Middle Ages resurrected in the 20th century. But do you know that the inhabitants of Kielce rose to the age-old bait?! Well, pretty soon a gang of young Poles gathered to attack the Jews. They were armed with sticks, stones, pipes, literally any crude weapon they could lay their hands on. When the police were called in, they actually aided and abetted the bloodthirsty hordes, so that soon enough, all the Jews in the building had been done to death in the most dreadful manner. Some had thrown themselves out of the windows in an effort to escape. All were unrecognizable.

"Yes, I think that this was the event which finally pushed me over the brink. Poland was not a place for Jews. This was my subconscious decision, but it took some time to implement. I spent the winter in Cracow and the summer in a sanatorium, Jelenia Gora, in Lower Silesia. When I finally left my homeland, I traveled for two days and nights to Switzerland. It

was difficult for a Jew to leave Poland at that time, for we were due to be commissioned into the Polish Army. There were many entanglements and difficulties to overcome. The fact was that I had a cousin in Switzerland who was urging me to come to Davos, to a sanatorium, to recover my health. At that time, I was still suffering from the aftereffects of malnutrition and diphtheria. So, I parted from aunt and uncle who eventually made their way to Bnei Brak. It was actually in Switzerland that I met your mother. She had an aunt in Switzerland, and she had come from London to stay with her for a while. Well, they

The Reifer's Wedding

happened to be visiting this aunt's friend in Basle, and someone who knew us both introduced us.

"We were both alone in the world. We had both been through Gehinnom. We were like pieces of driftwood on a vast sea, tossed together — but this is the way of Providence. This was meant to be. She brought me to London, for she was based there at that time. She had been living with a cousin and working in the West End.

"All these years, your mother and I have been simply unable to look one another in the eye and divulge our stories to one another. Rather, we have built up pictures from hints and guesswork. It is far easier to look away, to carry one's own burden with one's eyes to the ground."

"So your story ends here!"

"Well, judge for yourself. The answer is 'yes' and 'no.' The boundaries of any human story are arbitrary, are they not? Yes, the story of my war experiences and their immediate aftereffects ends here. But, then again, perhaps it continues, in you and with you.

"Certainly, the war has taught me many harsh lessons, not to be dependent on anyone, for one thing. You may find this a strange statement, but you see, before the war I was part of a family of four children.[6] My destiny was clearly mapped out for me. I would follow in my father's footsteps, and my grandfather's, and his father's before him. It was a safe, if narrow world. But I knew exactly what I was and what I was meant to be. Then this huge catastrophe happened, which no human mind could foresee, and blew all that utterly to bits. I had seen the very worst human behavior, people changing allegiance at their own convenience, human beings who were no more elevated than members of the animal kingdom. If I am being a little ambiguous, so be it, for I include in these

---

6. My brother Moshe Dov perished in Bunclau in Czechoslovakia.

categories not only our tormentors, but also unfortunately some members of our own race. This was 'their' plan, and this is what they reduced some of our Jews to, as well. Things were done over there that were never done before or since. It is not for us to apportion blame, for in that kingdom of darkness and despair, anything was possible. Yet, I had also seen the best, the noblest and the finest to which a human being can aspire. And this is the paradox.

"What we had also witnessed, all of us who survived the cataclysm, was the nature of Jewish history itself. There is a Midrash which states that when the Torah was given on Mount Sinai, sinah (hatred) descended to the world. This is anti-Semitism. It is a blind, irrational hatred, which admits no boundaries. What motivated the mob that stormed the refuge of the seventy-six Jews in Kielce? This took place, let us not forget, a year after the greatest, most calculated slaughter of Jews in human history, most of which had been enacted on Polish soil. Yet, the Moloch is insatiable. It demands more and more sacrifices. There is something more at work here. What we see in our history is something beyond any finite human understanding, for even in the darkest holes, if we but wish to, we can see something more powerful at work — Providence, the Hand of G-d.

"And then, there is the miracle that came later, in our own lifetimes. This, too, affirms the same principle. When we were liberated, when we crawled out of the hellholes of Europe, we were like the prophet Ezekiel's bodies with flesh and sinews, but not living. We emerged from a literal valley of 'dry bones' but we did not truly belong to the 'living' camp. There were those, then, who said 'avdah tikvasenu,' we have lost all hope of Jewish survival, of the future of our people. But just look what has happened within fifty years! A rebirth and revitalization, beyond human expectation. Yes, Hitler lies rotting beneath his bunker but the people he attempted to expunge, to relegate to a 'civilization of the museum' has outlived him. It is in such broad brushstrokes on a vast canvas that we must see our own experiences. After all, our 'little lights' have their day and then fade into nothingness. But all that I have tried to tell you has to be seen in both contexts, that of the individual, in this case myself, and the larger context, that of our eternal nation. And this is the principle reason why our stories, even though the telling is painful, are for posterity, and for those generations yet to come."

It was with these words that my father concluded his story, some weeks after we had made so tentative a beginning.

"But Father," I ask him finally. "The story has been told so many times. The camps, the appels, the beatings, the gassings, that, G-d forgive me and young people of my generation, we find the details banal ... How shall I describe it ... Where is the chiddush?"

"The chiddush? No, it is true, there is none here, or nothing that you can ever imagine of the first time the doors of the first cattle car you ever rode in were creakingly slid open and you were driven out into daylight and a world that seemed at first glance like a vast lunatic asylum. But a chiddush to the world ten or twenty or thirty years on? Everything loses its novelty as it becomes told or remembered, so even this is in danger of undergoing the same process of absorption into our daily consciousness, losing forever the power to shock. But listen, why should MY story not be told, my story or your mother's story? Is it any less valid, any less worthy of being told than a hundred, a thousand other such stories? In the famous words of the Haggadah: 'He who expounds lengthily on "the story" is even more *praiseworthy!' It is the act of telling which is in itself significant, no matter how many times the story has been told or by whom.*

"I know many Holocaust stories have been written, but each one merits being told. I am getting older, and as I reach the white-haired years, which as a boy shivering on some filthy straw pallet in Gerlitz I had never thought to see, I think, 'And why me?' This is the question which occurs to every Holocaust survivor with monotonous regularity, 'Why was I kept alive, while millions of others perished?' Since the A-mighty runs His world with purpose, and of that I remain more convinced, and not less, I must fulfill that purpose, in telling the world what happens when humanity replaces belief in G-d with belief in the 'purity of race.' What we saw with our own eyes was the inversion of everything noble and G-d-like in man. Our lives became disposable, things to be 'organized' away with fanatical zeal because we did not fit into their plan."

"Then, at last, I began to see my father in a new light. I began both to be able to place his personality in the broader context which he had spoken of, and to see him for what he had been, a frail, lonely youth, broken both physically and emotionally by his years of suffering. This he still was, beneath the semblance of the elderly man. This was a process at once illuminating and painful, when one begins to see one's parents as the composite people, which they really are, instead of 'parents,' those unchanging and unchangeable icons of our childish imaginations. And gradually, too, I realized that the doubts and uncertainties which had hung over us in childhood had been resolved by his narration, and this was deeply moving and satisfying. It was like finally fitting the missing pieces of a massive jigsaw puzzle into their proper places."

MOTHER'S
STORY

The Inky-blue Tattoo

By now, I had accomplished half of what I had set out to do. I had heard my father's story and I had visited Poland. But there still remained the other half — my mother's story.

This I approached with extreme caution, for what had happened to her, in my childish imagination, had always appeared to me the more horrific. She had been briefly in Auschwitz – albeit briefly.[1] The very name conjured up a picture of the worst that human life has to offer. It was as if there was some sort of academy of human suffering, and Auschwitz was at the top of the list. The inky-blue tattoo on her forearm, which she had never attempted to conceal, had been the frequent subject of our childhood musings. Yet, in the matter of human suffering, once my parents had decided to speak out, my mother often deferred to my father. "You know, your father spent six years in different lagers," and this fact, seemingly canceled out her 'superiority' at having been in Auschwitz.

There were certain effects on my mother's methods of parenting, too, which were all too apparent. Do not get the wrong impression. My mother was never, as you might imagine, the classic, possessive mother. She did not seek to protect us from an outer world projected as an inherently perilous place. She never said, "It's too cold, too dark, don't go alone." She never waited transfixed in a certain position, for our homecomings from school. No, she taught us

---

1. Mother had been imprisoned briefly in Auschwitz for the first time, but for over a month the second time.

independence and self-reliance at a young age. She sent us alone to school and on errands. If there was fear of the 'vast unknown' of the world as she had experienced it, as a darkly inhuman place, she never betrayed it. No, looking back, I think that if we felt effects they were, in fact, quite the opposite ones of what you might expect, not depressed, not pessimistic. On the contrary, she was cheerfully ambitious, hardworking, conscientious — striving for excellence in every sphere of her life. This is something she instilled in us thoroughly. "The way to 'win,' to become a 'somebody,' is through hard work. Make no mistake about it. By slacking, by shirking, you will never reach the 'top of the ladder.'" And to this end she pushed and cajoled us. She would ask us interminable questions about what we had learned in school that day. Were there any difficulties with our work? "Take out your books — I will help you. French? Yes, I will test you. Mathematics? Let's have a look ... I think your standard is dropping a little in such and such. I will speak to Father — it may be necessary to hire a private tutor for a while."

Such methods continued throughout my youth, and if Mother argued with teachers, hired private tutors, cajoled me step by step onward, her aim was altogether something larger. She was vigilant, being on her guard constantly for any falling off, wanting us to shine like the brightest stars in the constellation. It was as if she were saying, "Success equals security." Or, "If you succeed, you are vindicating all that we lost, proving to Hitler that we are still around, and mean to climb to the top again. Each step of the way is hard, so hard, but we are determined." Yet, sometimes we longed for a more relaxed attitude, a chance to be just ourselves, just children, not to have anything to prove, no axe to grind.

Dispossessed, humiliated, brutalized, outcast ... these were words it remained difficult to associate with Mother. Yet, having said that, there were moments when we saw a passing *flicker of fear. In those seconds her demeanor changed, she became again the suffering young girl she must have been. But had we imagined it? For as swiftly as clouds skittering across a graying sky, her expression changed. It was gone, evaporated like morning dew and all we saw was the bright, optimistic mother we knew so well.*

I knew instinctively, before I heard one word of her story, that hers would be intrinsically different than Father's. His was a man's way of looking at the war, facts and figures and a detached, almost philosophical stance. Mother talked much of faith as we were growing up. "Go, my children, with the A–mighty's help, and come back safely." Had she felt this when in Auschwitz? It was an obvious question — and a dangerous one too.

"Mother, before we begin, the first question I want to ask you is, did you not feel forsaken by G-d and man in Auschwitz?"

"You may think that this sounds strange, but no, we felt His presence so much more. He was, oh, how shall I explain it, with us at every step of the way. We never, G-d forbid, blamed G-d. No, we knew that this was a man-made evil, and that in a world where G-d gives people the choice to act as they will, it is always possible that they will create an Auschwitz. But we saw Him in so many ways, in a starving girl giving away her soup ration to a friend who was dying, in finding some moments to pray from a siddur which was freely circulated among the girls, in managing to fast on Yom Kippur. We were so close to death there (death could come at any second, it was our constant companion), that paradoxically, we saw G-d more clearly too. I know people say that there was no strength to think of anything beyond one's piece of bread, and there were those who, sadly, fell to the level of animals, but we tried so hard to rise above this. It

was partly self-preservation, because we knew very well that if we would lose the tzelem Elokim (the G-dly image) we would have granted our enemies their victory, there and then, on a platter. It was so hard, harder than anything you can imagine. Everything there was hard — even the simplest things we take for granted."

"There was another part to the question — did you feel forsaken by man?"

"By man! Yes, a very definite yes. We were 'taken' away during the final phases of the war. You know that Hungarian Jewry was one of the last to be deported. We had very little introduction to the Nazis. Your father lived through years of hell in the ghetto — so that by the time he got to the concentration camps, in a manner of speaking, he had already been initiated in their methods. The lager was just an extension of the ghetto — the logical conclusion, if you like. But we, in Hungary? We were not exactly living in a 'fool's paradise.' We heard rumors, persistent rumors — and we were living in fear, a terrible fear that our turn would come. (You know that sometimes the fear of a certain situation is worse than actually facing it when it comes.)

"As the war in Europe progressed, Hungary became a haven for Jews. Our regent, Miklos Horthy, was then a man in his 70's. When the Germans invaded Hungary in March, 1944, Horthy was restricted but not yet under house arrest. Several members of the Hungarian government, cooperating with Eichmann who had taken up residence in the Majestic Hotel in Budapest, began to implement a virulent anti-Jewish policy. Within a matter of weeks life for the Jews changed.[2]

---

2. Eichmann began from this point onward swiftly and efficiently to round up the Jews from every town, except Budapest, so that by July, 1944, there was not a man, woman or child to be found in all the provinces (except those few in hiding). By July, Horthy regained a little more power and, with the assistance of the neutral countries like Sweden, he managed to expel Eichmann to Vienna.

The Germans were furious. Horthy retaliated by calling on the army, even the

*"All the anti-Jewish laws, which in other countries they
had had months, years to get used to, were slapped on us one
after another."*

"And now — to your story ..."
*"Yes, I suppose the time has come. Did you know that I
kept a diary of my experiences? I was a young girl, living at
home, comfortable, protected, when the war started. I wrote
down my feelings as things went from bad to worse. I wrote
about my childhood, too, and how things, up to then, had been
almost idyllic. When they came to take us away, I hid it, with
some other valuables. After the war, I went back with a friend
and searched my house for these things. The house had been
completely ravaged by Russian and Romanian soldiers in
transit. It was unrecognizable. There were heaps of rubbish
everywhere in which I could identify old photographs and
other familiar items. Incredibly, some of the objects in the
hiding place were still there. One of these was my diary."*

Dear Diary,

I have decided to keep this record, because I know that the things
we are going through now are quite exceptional. One day, they may
even be counted as history. Also, it helps me to get through each day
better if I have someone in whom to confide. Let me introduce
myself to you. My name is Edith Schattin, known to my friends as
Ditta. We live in the town of Sarospotok, in Hungary. This is neither
a village nor a big town. I would say that it is something in between.

Jewish Brigade, and attempting a coup, but in this he failed and was put under virtual
house-arrest.
Szálesi became prime minister, and treatment of Jews again worsened with Jews in
Budapest being arrested and thrown into the Danube. Some were also rounded up and
taken on death marches, heading towards Austria. After the war, the Red Army took over
Hungary.

Sarospotok is situated in the Carpathian mountain region of Hungary. On all sides you can see snow-capped peaks, even in spring, and the vineyards creep up the side of the mountains. I imagine parts of Italy look like this. The famous 'Tohaly wine' is producal here. Everything is defined by the mountains. As soon as you step out of your house, it seems as though the mountains are rising from the bottom of your very street, though of course they are much farther away than one imagines.[3]

Sarospotok, although small in population, is quite a prestigious place. It is known as a 'Kalturstadt,' for the many colleges and centers of education there. In fact, it possessed the only English boarding school in the region with house masters from England, and sons of the titled nobility as pupils.

Our family owns a wholesale and retail grocery store in Sarospotok. The store also has a hardware department, and meets the post-office requirements. We sell things having to do with the

Father - Gershon Eliezer Schattin

vineyards, like straw to bind the vines, spray for the grapes, and also drinks in barrels. The store was established by my great-grandfather. From my grandfather, it was passed down to my father, Gershon Eliezer Schattin. He is an excellent businessman, but we all think he is a little over-conscientious. For example, he opens the shop at 5:30 in the morning, and, as he acts as his own accountant, he is busy until late at night with his books. Our shop, so it is said, was the very first to open in our town — and it is still in business. Father has a decidedly different way of doing business. He tells his employees to give overweight rather than under-

---

3. Sometimes we would hire a horse and cart and ascend to the top of the mountains. When you reach the highest point, there is a small, mirror-like lake. Every so often, we would travel to the next town and go up into the mountains from there. The scenery is absolutely breathtaking.

My mother's parents, Reb Noson Rechnitzer and his wife. The young child is my mother.

weight. He never buys shoddy goods, and is always prepared to pay a little extra for quality. It's funny, but he always knows what to buy, what will sell. All the other shopkeepers in town come to him to ask if he happens to have bought such and such an item. If he has, they take it for a sign, and then they go and buy it too. Well, that's my father.

Now to my mother, for I must introduce her, too. Mother comes from a bigger town, where they had a beautiful house with all the modern conveniences and labor-saving devices. She spent part of her youth in Hamburg and Vienna. She is intelligent, educated and talented. Sometimes, I catch a certain sadness in her eyes. Is it only my imagination? I feel she is not truly fulfilled in the 'small-town' life and longs to return to the more sophisticated city life which she has known. Of course, I have never questioned her about this directly. It is just a feeling I get sometimes, but there again, I could be wrong. She is my 'best' friend, and I have absolutely no secrets from her. Everyone in Sarospotok, even the gentile neighbors, nod sagely at me as I pass and say, "Oh, we know your mother. She is a true lady."

Our house is quite a large building, situated at the corner of two intersecting streets. We have five rooms and a kitchen (which is attached to the shop, on the other side of the yard). Then there are three more rooms, which are for the use of my grandparents. Besides these eight rooms we have eight storerooms for goods for the shop. In the storerooms we keep barrels full of drinks, and sackfuls of dry goods such as flour and sugar, which are sold wholesale.

My mother keeps busy overseeing the household. Her duties are many and various. For example, several days a week, she has to make trips to the market to buy vegetables, or to the butcher. On these trips, she is always accompanied by our maid or an employee of the shop, who helps to carry home the heavy baskets. You can imagine that this is quite a time-consuming and tiring business. Of course, she meets 'everyone' there and stops to speak with Mrs. So and so, or Mrs. So and so. She is friendly with everyone and inquires about their welfare. They, in turn, recognize that she is a lady and that she would never 'stoop' to engage in gossip. As for the housework, the maids do the washing, laundry and other tasks. Mother also has a Jewish cook, Mrs. Trotner, whom she oversees carefully, so that although the cook's responsibilities are weighty, most of the hard physical work is carried out by others. She bakes

*Mother - Sara
Rechnitzer Schattin*

bread, challos, and endless, fragrant yeast cakes.

Our house is always busy, with guests in constant supply. Usually these are *bochurim* from the local yeshivah. As for me, there have been times when I used to complain that I had no time to do my homework, because I was always helping in the shop. But this was in the good old days, when everything was still 'normal.' (Why, oh why did it all have to change?) In any case, I always managed to do well at school, and I say this without boasting. I had to study very intensely to do well; of the thirty-two girls in my

class, only four were Jewish, and two of the four managed to grad-
uate with top marks at the end of the year.

The state was not responsible for the marking of our examinations.
It was the school itself which gave reports. They tried to spoil it for us
Jewish girls, and play down how well we really did. But we learned to
work even harder, and, in the end, they just had to be fair! Perhaps,
even then, this was the start of the 'Jewish problem,' these little day-to-
day things. I don't know. We were always taught at home that things
would get better, and that our troubles would dissipate with the wind.
But you see, they didn't. In fact, they gradually became worse.

As I write now, when the war in Europe has already begun, I
think back to how naïve we were then. Do you think that one day
we will think that things, as they are now, are comparatively
'good'? Is there nothing sure in the world anymore?

Yours,
Ditta.

Dear Diary,

You remember the 'unpleasantness' I mentioned at the end of
my last entry? Well, I am sorry to have to report that it has not gone
away. Once upon a time, life consisted of school, friends, helping in
the shop, running errands for Mamma and Pappa, all pleasant
things. Of course, we had our little worries, but they were just little worries. I can see that now. I discussed the situation with my
two best friends, and they feel the same as I do. At school, the word
'Jew' was often bandied about in some context or other. We are constantly being picked on by the teachers, although we, two of the
Jewish girls, always had top marks.

This year, part of Czechoslovakia was returned to Hungary, and
many of my father's friends were called up to join the army. My
father was renowned for having a first class-business brain, and he
was chosen to distribute groceries to the whole county. Due to this
service, he was never called up to be a soldier.

Still, about this army business, I remember hearing that my maternal grandfather had lost most of his money in government bonds. His only son spent the entire war in the army. And then they say that the 'Jews have never been patriots.'

Grandfather was a remarkably honest man. After World War I, when the communists came, a delegation approached him to requisition all the wheat flour he used for making bread. Their leader had a high regard for grandfather and wanted to help him, so he said loudly, "Your son's flat has nothing in it. It's a waste of time looking there."

My grandfather, however, replied, "Yes, there is flour in my son's house."

Afterwards he told his family what he had said. They were all appalled. Grandfather calmly said, "If you want to hide things, don't tell me, because I will NOT tell a lie." He also lost a court case in which a woman had owed a considerable sum of money. The case was nearly won, but after all the evidence was presented and he was asked to take the oath, he drew himself up to his full height and proclaimed, "Never for money!"

After that, the judge used to greet him on the street, bowing deeply and lifting his hat.

But this is all by the way, and I return to the more recent past and our troubles.

Well, a few weeks ago, things really seemed to come to a head. One day, two plain-clothed detectives came into the shop.

"Who is in charge here?" they asked me in clipped tones.

"My father," I managed to stammer.

"Well, go and get him, young lady, we'd like a word with him."

Father came out of the back, where he had been hard at work on his books.

"Sir, we must ask you whether you sell matches in this shop."

"Yes, I do. Here they are, a whole shelf full. How many packets would you like?"

"I'm afraid that we must requisition all these matches."

Father shrugged his shoulders. Strange things happened every day now. If they wanted the matches, so be it, let them take them.

Two days later I was ill in bed with a high fever and my mother was watching over me. I fell into a feverish nightmare. I dreamed that Father had been arrested, by the very same plain-clothed detectives who had visited the shop the other day. I saw them putting a hand on his rounded, defeated shoulder and saying, "You must come with us now to the police station for questioning!" I saw the charcoal gray of their raincoats and the rigid set of their unsmiling features.

I awoke drenched in sweat and trembling.

At that moment — I am sure it was at that very moment — I heard a disturbance, which seemed to be issuing from the shop. (The shop was in fact an extension of the house itself, and consisted of two rooms, with two entrances from two different streets, one of which was the storehouse packed with items such as dry goods and drinks.)

A few minutes later, my mother tapped on my door. Her features were as white as the wall of my bedroom. "It's your father. He's been arrested."

"The dream, I dreamed it," I whispered half to myself.

It seems that Father had again been visited by two detectives asking for matches. When he said that he had none, they had simply arrested him.

By evening, the house was filled with friends and neighbors, and we were able to get a clearer picture of what had happened. It seems that all the well-to-do Jews of the town had been arrested on that day. Some were given a reason, others no reason at all. Later, they were told that their 'crime' was that they had sent money to the Czechs. My feeling is that they didn't need a reason to arrest them. It was something that 'they' had wanted to do for a long time. Some of them were beaten about, and then they were frog-marched through the streets to be taken to the next biggest town. Stones were thrown at them. Can you imagine the humiliation? All these loyal, good citizens … The next day, still in bed, I was visited by a gentile school friend. She told me gleefully, "You know, your daddy fainted on his march through the streets." But then, I had always had the feeling that she was an anti-Semite. (This started happening all the time, by the way, the real anti-Semites coming out of the woodwork.)

Later, we found out that Father had been taken to Budapest along with the others. There they had all been locked up. Can you believe me when I say that what followed were the worst weeks of my whole life? Well, Mother cried and cried. She would not touch food. She must have lost twenty pounds. After about three weeks, and a lot of string-pulling, the men were finally allowed home. Father arrived home one spring evening. He was pale and haggard and had aged about a hundred years. He sat down at our kitchen table and promptly burst into tears. Dear diary, I had never, ever seen my father cry!

Sorry for bringing you such sad stories, but there seems little else to tell nowadays.

Yours,
Ditta.

Dear Diary,

Perhaps it is good that I can write down all these things. Perhaps other 14-year-old girls in different parts of Europe are writing down the same things. But what I want to know is, when will it all be over? If we could see an end to it, I wouldn't mind so much. I want just once more, to pack a picnic and go with my parents and my brother to some quiet spot in the mountains and inhale the fresh, free air. Will that ever happen again? I wonder …

Dear Diary,

It was mostly bad news the last time I wrote, but I'm afraid there is more and more. We used to be so happy. I was a young girl from an ordinary family. My biggest problem ever was getting a bad mark on my exams and so making my dear, precious mother unhappy. Also, I was wondering when I would get to leave Sarospotok and see the wide world which my mother so often described. As we are an Orthodox family, we keep to ourselves here in Sarospotok, and mix with others like us, but we have always been on good terms with the gentiles. Now, it seems like we have stepped into a hall of distorting mirrors in which you see yourself completely distorted. Everything is the same, yet nothing is the same. Can anyone understand this? I look at the mountains now, those beautiful, inspiring mountains which always gave me such joy, and think of the verse in *Tehillim*, "I lift my eyes to the mountains, from whence comes my help? My help is from the L-rd, the Maker of Heaven and Earth."

Do you know how long has passed since I last wrote? It must be two months, and so much happened in between. One night, we all went to bed early and fell into a deep sleep. Suddenly, we heard a terrific knocking on the door. I glanced at my alarm clock. It was 2 in the morning. Mother and Father were already up. Gray-faced, they hurried downstairs. Again, plain-clothed policemen. They ordered my father to get dressed. Poor Father! He is still not completely over his first ordeal. *Ribbono Shel Olam*, what do they want from him now? Can't they see that he's a graying middle-aged man who is trembling from fear for himself and his family? Well, this time we received news that Father was arrested with a great number of other Jewish men, and they were all due to be taken to Siberia, in Russia. My father, who had never been a soldier, and who was nearly 50 years old, could never hope to survive the biting Russian winter.

I had a terrible eye infection and was not supposed to do any close work. But that night, after sobbing for about two hours without stopping, I took out Father's extra warm socks. He had bought them during one really severe winter that he had spent in Budapest. They needed darning, so I sat up stitching them until the first light of dawn began to appear over the mountains. In the morning, I ran to a shop to buy some special warm boots for him. Mother was so heartbroken. It was as if all her vital energies had been drained from her, and she was simply paralyzed. We left her looking out from the front window of our house, towards the mountains, dry-eyed. She could not face

Noson (2 ½ years old) and Edith (5 years old)

seeing Father about to be marched away, so there was no help for it, we would have to go alone. I took my younger brother, Noson,[4] and we hurried to the police station.

Again, the men were marched through the streets of Sarospotok as if in disgrace. Father had a heavy suitcase with him, so we helped him to carry it. Would you believe it? This time I saw it with my own eyes. There was a mob lining the pavements, shouting anti-Semitic slogans at these poor men. Some faces in the crowd were familiar to me. They were customers who used to come into the shop. A woman tugged at my sleeve, it was my piano teacher. There was real grief in her eyes as she spoke in a whisper, "Edith, I am so sorry. I, we ... simply cannot explain what is happening." By now the mob had taken to throwing stones. We left my father reluctantly, and ran home to see how Mother was. She must have managed to pull herself together, for she had left us a note. "I have gone to see if anything can be done for us." Her plan worked. A first cousin of my father's, Bela Kornitzer, a famous author and journalist, and other well-known personalities who were good friends of Father's, spoke up for him. After five long days, Father was sent home.

We were overjoyed to see him, but each time this happened, we had the feeling that this was not the end of our troubles. This is how things are nowadays. One never knows what is just around the cor-

---

4. Noson had been named after my grandfather, Noson Rechnitzer. My grandfather was not a Rav but was held in such high esteem that he was buried in the Rabbinical section of the cemetery. Although a businessman, he spent every available moment in Torah study.

ner, ready to spring out at us, so one can never really be either happy or sad. We are full of fear, a fear that gnaws at your very bones.

Yours,

Ditta

Dear Diary,

Well, what is my news? Every day, trainloads of Polish Jews and Jews of other nationalities pass through our railway station on their way to the camps. Ours is a typically pleasant provincial station, with its neat benches and hanging baskets, framed by the tall chestnut trees beyond.

These Polish Jews are a huddle of men, women and children of all ages, shapes and sizes. They are dressed in a poor, ragged way. The women are usually headscarfed and bowed. But the worst thing is that they look so passive, so defeated. We try to run down to the station with bits of food for them. I am so frightened, wondering if we are next. But in the back of my mind I feel that they are a very different kind of Jew. Surely, surely, this can never happen to us. Oh, but how wrong, how sinful to even think this way. Things are so confusing. What must the chestnut trees, swaying serenely in the wind, make of all this terrible human mess?

It was the festival of Sukkos, and we returned home from the synagogue. As I entered the house, I saw what to me was a most unusual, even shocking thing. I saw my mother with the telephone receiver in her hand![5] It seems that my uncle (my father's brother), who was a bank director in the largest bank in Eperjes, a town in Hungary, had been arrested, and was about to be deported for resettlement in the East. We had some idea what this term meant by now, as rumors had been flying thick and fast. We knew that it was a matter of life or

---

5. This is forbidden on a Jewish holiday.

death. My father eventually went down to the station to catch the first available train. He promised to be back by 10 o'clock that night. Accordingly, my brother and I waited the whole night for him at the taxi stand, and finally gave up at dawn. He did not turn up that night or the night after that. It was three days later when he arrived, thoroughly shaken by his ordeal. He had been removed from the train on which he had been traveling, and told quite bluntly, "Jew, you can walk."

He did not think he would ever see any of us again. What my father had managed to accomplish, however, was to get my uncle and his wife sent to a hospital in Budapest (where they remained from 1942 to 1944). But they are still on the lists for the camp. Somehow, I do not think that they will manage to stay free for long! Uncle Sándor Schattin was always such a hardworking man. That is how he managed to reach such a high position without working on the Sabbath. May G-d protect them both!

What a shock to the system! We had thought of the 'camps' before as a place where they sent those poor Polish Jews on the trains. Now, it was happening in our own family! Where will it end? Will we be safe anywhere?

I cry into my pillow every night. During the day I must put on a brave cheerful face, laugh, and even crack a few jokes. I must do this to keep my parents and my brother going, for I was always the cheerful one in the family. Inside I am churning with fear. Fear is something which never leaves us now. It is my secret life.

It is our secret life.

I remain yours,
Ditta

Dear Diary,

Trouble has a tendency to build up and all happen at once. 'It never rains,' the popular saying goes, 'it pours.' My younger brother, Noson, had been away from home for a few weeks. He was learning in my uncle OberRabbi Yaakov Deutsch's yeshivah, in Abaujszanto, when we received a phone call. By now, we had a tendency to view the phone more as an enemy than a friend! Well, it seems that Noson had quite suddenly developed scarlet fever. Scarlet fever is a very dangerous and infectious illness, and should you but mention it, everyone jumps from fright. The authorities demanded that he be sent home. They rang Mother, "Could you fetch your son home immediately? We just can't take the risk!" My parents hired a car and set out in the middle of the night to fetch him home. I sat all night on the edge of my bed and prayed to the A-mighty to send him home to us safe and sound. I know we argue quite often, but I do care for him deeply, truly I do. So I prayed: "Dear G-d, I promise I'll try not to quarrel with Noson in the future. Just send him home to us safe and sound!"

They had a terrible journey, but eventually arrived home. Later on, the sanitary officer called and insisted that the car be fumigated!

That was one incident. If you think, by the way, that our life sounds exciting, you're wrong! Another incident comes to mind. This time, it was actually a funny one. That was the night we thought we had burglars. My father and I had been ordered out of our house for a while, because of my brother's contagious condition, leaving Mother to nurse him. Since we sold foodstuffs, it was considered very perilous for us to remain in close contact with infectious disease. We were now living in a house whose owner was away in the army. His wife had rented the house to us, while she went to stay with her mother. Very late one night we heard a noise. My father and I picked up our shoes, ready to throw them out the window to attract attention, and some heavy sticks with which to tackle the burglars. Armed with these, we made our way downstairs, quaking in every limb. But whom do we see? None other than our landlady! She had lost her key, and was attempting to climb in through a downstairs window in order to retrieve it. As she was quite a portly lady, she was wedged somewhere halfway through. She could neither get in nor out again. We both burst out into shaky laughter. For once, the situation was truly comical, the landlady stuck in our window and we, in our night attire, armed with shoes and sticks.

(Our landlady must have been a little confused from all her worry, by the way. Her husband was now serving in the working-army in the Ukraine. Everyone knew that they used these men for the most dangerous operations — planting and picking mines, and carrying the wounded from the frontlines under heavy fire. They were not even given guns!)

But let's return to my brother's illness. At this time, my grandmother (my mother's mother) developed a serious illness. She was well over 80. My mother wanted desperately to travel to see her, but was not allowed to leave the house as she might carry infection. She had a strong feeling that my grandmother was dying. We received letters constantly about the seriousness of her condition. After a few weeks, Mother finally received permission to travel. She had hardly arrived at grandmother's house, when my father developed pneumonia. We decided not to tell Mother about this, because we knew how ill grandmother was. Sadly, within a week, grandmother died. My father had managed to get to the phone several times and speak to my mother even though he was so ill, so she suspected nothing. He had a very high fever, and I nursed him for a few days, changing the cold compresses three or four times a night. All that time, I had a cold and a slight fever myself.

To cap it all, a couple of policemen came to requisition part of our house, so that they could live there. I was desperate. There was no one to advise me. Mother was still away, and Father was in no condition to be bothered. What do you think I did? I had a bright idea. I ran all the way to the governor's house, and I sobbed out my story. After a long silence he said: "Go home and don't worry anymore, child. I shall give orders for you to be left in peace."

You know, sometimes I don't feel 14 anymore. I feel like an 80–year–old woman carrying life's heavy burden on her shoulders.

I try hard not to feel sorry for myself as others are suffering so much more, but at times my feelings simply overwhelm me.

Yours ever,
Ditta

Dear Diary,

More and more young men are being called up to the working army. On the way to their posts they stay in Hungary, and our town is one of their stops.

Just the other day a young fellow came into the shop. He was a bespectacled, typically academic type. He complained, "I have studied at university and gained qualifications. And just look at me now, doing the worst menial jobs. Was this what I studied so hard for?"

By the way, we never saw any of these young men returning from the frontiers!

We live in constant worry and fear. We have been forbidden to use our radios, and a few weeks ago we packed them away. Sometimes, late at night, we remove them and try to listen to the BBC's international broadcasts. Often the frequency is jammed, but sometimes we manage to hear news about how the war is going, and it gives us some hope. We pray for Hitler to lose the war, and for Europe to return to peace.

You know, I think that what really keeps us going are our strong religious beliefs. I still feel, despite all these troubles, that there is a pattern and a purpose in the world, and nothing happens without a very good reason. Before the war broke out, many Orthodox youths had left the ways of their fathers and gone astray. I used to think that only something earth shattering could change the situation!

A few weeks ago, Mother arranged for me to visit her hometown. She thought that it would be good for me to get away from the strained atmosphere in Sarospotok for a while. She reasoned that the war might break out at any moment in Hungary, and that then we wouldn't be going anywhere for a while. So at long last, the final arrangements were made and I set out. It was a somewhat tiresome train journey from Sarospotok, and I amused myself by looking out at the scenery, and observing the other people in the smoke-filled carriage. Oh, I do love my homeland so, I thought with a piercing stab. My family has lived here for generations, and this is our home. But then I recalled the looks in the eyes of the mob on that terrible day that Father had been arrested, and realized that — after all — we are in exile.

The journey took two days. Oh, and when we arrived, what excitement! I was fussed over by relatives of all descriptions! It felt like I had suddenly been turned back into a carefree teenager again. I visited two aunts who lived in two different towns, and met several of my cousins. However, the high hopes with which my mother had sent me, to see young Jews conducting themselves in a more proper way than in Sarospotok, were not realized. She knew how much relentless teasing I was always having to put up with for my religious beliefs, and at these times she would always encourage me by saying, "You will see, when you visit my hometown how different the youngsters are there!"

Now I was seeing for myself that, unfortunately, the situation in these towns was much the same. I used to lecture them, for I felt that they were committing grave sins. But the longer I stayed, the more I felt myself paradoxically being influenced in small and subtle ways.

Even here, there were hardships caused by the war in Europe. One of my married cousins ended up having to live apart from her husband, as he had been assigned to a specialized work unit in his hometown. (He had been allowed to stay on in Czechoslovakia as a 'privileged worker.') My relatives were also harboring a little girl — a grand niece from Yugoslavia. She is safe with them for the moment, but who knows how long the situation will hold out.[6]

---

6. This family was eventually 'reunited' in Auschwitz, where the father was gassed, because he had a toe missing. The little girl survived and made her way to Switzerland after the war.

Springtime came to the town where I was staying with my relatives. But this spring was hardly greeted with the usual cheerfulness. Everyone was on edge, for the news was far from good. One morning we awoke to the sound of clanking noises and heavy banging. We all ran to the window, where we saw immediately that the street was full of enormous vans and tank-mounted machine guns. Our worst nightmares had materialized in front of our eyes, for here was the long-feared German army, marching arrogantly into Hungary.

A neighbor, hurried in to us, "Perhaps things are not as bad as they look. Perhaps they are only passing through." But at the sound of German voices barking orders outside, her voiced trailed off uncertainly. No, we all knew exactly what this meant without having to articulate it to one another. This is the end, each one of us screamed silently, an end to any springtime of freedom or hope!

Apart from that, I was many miles from home, dear diary! Only you can imagine how I felt.

I telephoned my parents and they asked me to return immediately. Of course, this was not so simple. Had this not been wartime, what an adventure it would have been!

After much discussion, an older cousin[7] was designated to accompany me. We got on a train which would take me home via Budapest. Every few hours our papers were checked, but they were always found to be in order. We arrived in Budapest and then had to change trains. We placed our luggage on the racks, and took our seats and waited. But the train did not move. It spluttered a little, made a few perfunctory hissing sounds, but then lapsed into total silence. By now, it was clear that there was some sort of rumpus going on around the station. My cousin was a few years older than I was, but still just a youngish boy. He decided that we should investigate. We got off the train and passed through a side entrance into the street. We were, so it seemed, safe now, but hearing a com-

---

7. This cousin survived the war. His father, however, went to search for him and was shot and thrown into the Danube.

motion, curiosity got the better of him. "Let's go back to the main entrance, there we'll get an idea what's really going on?!" So, off we went. As we passed through the ornate portals, and I hardly believe it myself, we were arrested by two policemen, and taken to Budapest's Gestapo headquarters. We were frog-marched in. I glanced at my cousin, but he looked as white and shaken as I must have looked. We were separated immediately. I was sent with the women and children. Soon, a Hungarian gendarme arrived to take our details. He asked my date of birth, and then turned to his colleague and muttered under his breath, "Why, she is just a child." I had the feeling then that he was only acting under German orders, and perhaps there was still hope for us.

Then we were all taken outside to wait in the pouring rain. Luckily, I was wearing a warm coat, rainhat, and suitable shoes. But how I cried at this indignity, my tears mingling with the raindrops on my cheeks! A-mighty G-d, let me be back home with dear Mamma and Pappa and my brother Noson.

Night fell and we were finally allowed back inside. We were shown into bare cells. It took a while for us to realize that we were supposed to sleep on the floor. An elderly woman who had told me that I reminded her of her daughter pleaded with me to lie on her lap to sleep. All night, she stroked my hair gently, with infinite tenderness. In this way, we provided some comfort to one another.

By the morning, the women were all terribly depressed.

"We are lost," they cried. I tried to console them, "Don't talk like that. Things may not be so bad. They will free us soon, you will see."

"Poor child," they turned to look at me pityingly, the sun from the tiny barred windows just beginning to slant off their haggard features. "Don't you know what this means, when they gather women and children together? Haven't you heard of the concentration camps and the gas chambers, or how they throw Jews into the Danube here?"

"Leave her be," said another, "if she does not know, she will learn soon enough!" and she gave me the look that a monitor at a boarding school might cast an innocent new pupil.

However, nothing they said could shake my belief that I would return home. My biggest worry was that the anxiety and uncertainty would break my poor mother's heart.

So I kept on repeating the words, like an incantation: "We shall be free by the weekend, you will see!"

A gentile lady, who had been arrested by mistake, was told that she would now be released. So I seized my opportunity to smuggle a letter to my parents with her.

I had brought along a little food for the journey and I tried to make this last as long as possible, but by the third day, it was all gone. I had vowed not to eat the prison meals as they were not kosher. But on that day, a strange thing happened. No food arrived. Now we were all sure that we would be starved to death. Yes, this is what they had planned for us. My imagination ran riot. I imagined myself screaming for food. I imagined myself weakened and lying on the floor, and the Germans letting gas into the room. I recited the *Al cheit* prayer which we say on Yom Kippur, for I felt that my end was near. Just then, news filtered through into our cell that tomorrow some of us would be released. Suddenly, we all sat up straighter and brushed down our crumpled clothing. It was like a ray of sunshine in the darkness of night. The next day, an official read out the names of the lucky ones to be set free. My name, Schattin, came toward the end of the list. How my heart beat and pounded, like the waves of a stormy sea.

"Does this mean that I may I travel home?" I asked the official naively?

"Yes, if you want to be released. Of course, if not, we could always accommodate you a little longer," he replied in sarcastic tones.

That was not the end of my troubles, for it took me ages to get home, on my own, in an occupied country.

Yours,

Ditta

Dear Diary,

When I left the prison, I realized that I was completely stranded. I did not know where to go, or to whom to turn. I felt so completely alone and lost. In some ways, I had always been sheltered.

A few yards down the road from the prison I noticed a 'phone box.' First, I tried contacting a number of distant relatives. One was my uncle's brother. My uncle was a Rav in Grosswardein.[8] His brother was Dr. Deutsch,[9] the director of the Jewish high school which had been requisitioned by the Germans for their headquarters. Dr. Deutsch had four daughters. Little did I know that the girls had been put to work washing floors for the Germans. At last I got through to them. The girls warned me, "Do not come here, the Germans have taken over the school!" I felt a sense of terrible foreboding pierce through me. Then, I tried making some other calls, but there was no answer at any of the numbers. At last, I managed to get in touch with a distant relative, a nerve specialist (head of the Hospital of Nervous Diseases) and his family. He remained in Budapest throughout the war because the Germans had need of his skills. They told me not to worry, and gave me detailed directions to their house. When I arrived, they insisted that I spend Shabbos with them. By now, I was able to speak to my parents, and they sent special papers to help me get home. Mother had also baked a special cake in celebration of my release, which arrived with my papers. Shabbos was a joyous occasion, but it all passed in a blur of excitement and fatigue — the freshly-starched cloth, the candles and, above all, the heady mixture of freedom.

As soon as Shabbos ended, a policeman, posing as my father, arrived to escort me home. This was not so simple. While I was away, many new laws had been issued against the Jews. One was that no Jew was allowed to be on the streets after 9 p.m. How on

---

8. He had been chosen from three candidates to be the 'Rav' (Rabbi) of one of the largest Orthodox synagogues, that of Grosswardein. We were supposed to go to his induction, but at that point the Germans invaded so he remained Rav in Abaujszanto where he had his own yeshivah.

9. Dr. Deutsch later became a member of the Knesset in Israel.

earth was I to get home? The streets were crowded with policemen buzzing like bees around a honey pot. On the way to Budapest's main station, we were stopped at least three times. By the time I got onto the train, I cannot describe to you how fast my heart was beating. "Move, move," I willed the train to start. At last, it burst into movement. "Only a few more hours and I will see them all." Oh, how I prayed as the train chugged onward, with a faster and faster rhythm. Suddenly, there was a tremendous hubbub outside our compartment door. The door was flung open and the sound of raucous laughter reached us. It was a group of young policemen, who were obviously slightly drunk.

"May we join you, young lady," they inquired in exaggeratedly courteous tones. Each utterance was met with peals of coarse merriment by the others. A sickly smell of alcohol filled the carriage and hung on the stale air.

"Home, home," my heart pounded, as if this was some kind of spell to ward off evil.

At long last, we reached our dear hometown of Sarospotok. The tears rolled down my cheeks unchecked as I saw the familiar sign. But the danger was not quite over, for here, too, there was a strict curfew on Jews.

However, in a little over half an hour, we reached my parents' front door. Dear Diary, how can I ever describe the way my parents looked as I entered the house? They appeared so pained and broken, altogether somehow smaller and frailer than I had imagined. The only one who looked the same was my brother Noson, and for once, I was glad of his cheerfulness. How I had dreamt of this moment of homecoming, with my family shedding tears of joy to see me. Oh, I would sleep for days, and eat just what I liked! I was free! Or so I thought! For the sad truth is that none of us were free anymore. Can you understand this? I hardly understand it myself. While in prison, I thought often, "What crime have we committed?" But it seems that we were born Jews, and that was enough. Again, I ask you, can you understand this? Can anyone explain this to me? Has the whole world gone mad?

Truly it is only the One Above who can help us now.

Yours devotedly,

Ditta

⧼⧽

Dear Diary,

Well, the Germans have certainly gotten down to work, issuing new laws every day. You hardly get used to one rule, and lo and behold, another law has been proclaimed. The latest thing is that we are only allowed out of doors until 7 at night, and now we all have to sew a large, yellow star on our lapel. I didn't mind this, dear diary, truly I didn't, for I am not ashamed to be a Jew — but the reason they did this was simply to humiliate us. Another thing they did was force us to pay them large sums of money. They also arrested men and even women, and tortured them until they would tell where they had hidden their jewelry and other valuables. We are so afraid that they will come for Pappa. All our nerves are frayed to the breaking point. I really don't think we can take much more!

Last week was Pesach. I had always loved Pesach in particular, as it is such a great family occasion. We sat down to the *Seder* table and for once, we had all determined to set aside our fears. We recited the '*Ho Lachma Anya*,' the opening recitation, and each word seemed to speak to our hearts. Suddenly, the sirens sounded. One by one each of the family got up and left the table. And do you know what I did? I sat on at the table and continued singing at the top of my voice '*Ma Nishtanah*.' I sang "Why is this night different than other nights?" But there was no one to answer my question, only the incessant wail of the sirens. "Hold on," I thought "hold on to this very moment, this reality, for who knows if what is coming will not be worse."

So Pesach passed, and the very next day our community leader was called in by the Germans. We had noticed, too, that fresh police reinforcements had arrived in town. The streets were buzzing with policemen. Dear Diary, we are just like butterflies waiting to be trapped! We wait and wait for news every day. What is it they want from us now?

Perhaps, they will stop at our money, perhaps it is things they want, and not people. This hope keeps us going from day to day.

I'll write again.

Yours,
Ditta

Dear Diary,

Several days have passed, so I will continue the story. Well, the day our community leader was arrested, we were waiting with bated breath for news of him. We thought that this would some-how signal to us what was going to happen to the rest of us. But there was no news. We had a orphaned gentile girl called Celia liv-ing with us for the past few months. The previous girl who lived with us had stayed ten years. She had come to us straight from her foster parents, and Mother had personally arranged her wedding, even cooking and baking for it. Both of these girls love my mother dearly and are very attached to the rest of the family. Well, Celia was getting exceedingly worried on our behalf. She decided to go out and make some inquiries. The hours passed and it was 9 o'clock, 9:30, then 10 o'clock. We all sat in our comfortable lounge, listening to the heavy chiming of our grandfather clock. It was half-past 10, and by now, you could hear a pin drop in the room. No one spoke. Even my normally bubbly brother had lapsed into a heavy, uneasy silence. At last, the sound of footsteps returning. Celia entered the room, sobs shaking her entire frame. We watched her thin shoulders rise and fall convulsively. She had not dared to come back home for a long time, for she simply did not know how to break the news to us.

We waited a while, then we burst out together. "Celia, dear, tell us, tell us, what you have managed to discover," we all cried with one voice.

"I can't tell," she insisted. "I can't." But then in a steadier voice,

"Well, they say that tomorrow morning you will all be taken away. You may pack a parcel weighing fifty kilograms, but that is all."

Mother rose from her seat.

"Well, Celia, thank you very much. That seems to be all," she said. "I think I will just go and lie down in the other room. Thank you so much for all your efforts on our behalf and may the A-mighty Father in Heaven Who watches over us be with you always."

At this, she left the room.

We were all stunned into silence. I touched something wet on my cheeks and realized that I had been crying. As I turned to look at the pale, frightened face of my brother, my heart turned to stone: "Dear G-d in Heaven, they can't do this to us, they can't ."

"Hush, hush child," my father said, sensing my anger. "Perhaps you had best go and lie down like your mother."

Shivering, I lay down on my bed, and then I did something you might think a little strange. I pulled on my heavy boots, and lifted myself onto the snow-white bedding. I wanted to leave it dirty and soiled for them, just as 'they' had soiled our lives forever. The injustice of it all burned within me like a gnawing flame that would not be extinguished. I ought to have been packing, but it all seemed so hopeless. What would I be packing for? Would we ever be using the things we packed? I was always the strong one, but now I felt utterly forsaken. Questions whirled in my head: "Where will they take us? What will happen to us? What food would we have?" I had always been fond of bread, beans and potatoes, because these are staple foods that are very cheap in Hungary. Who would have dreamt that even these cheap foods would be now a luxury for us?

More things happened during the evening. We contacted our neighbors and passed on the news, but by then we could cry no more. We had spent all our tears. Later on, the same policeman who had brought me home from Budapest came to see us, but he could only confirm the worst. He offered to take whatever we wished to leave behind, with him. He also offered to take me and hide me as best he could. Of course, I refused. How could I be parted from my family? Father decided to give him our *Sefer Torah*, which had been in the family for generations, for safekeeping. It seemed that we had to part from everything that we most treasured. Later, when this policeman left, bearing the *Sefer Torah*, my father hid a few valuables in a special place in the chimney, which he then bricked up again. These consisted of the few pieces of jewelry that were left to us now, and some silverware. (The gold watch, however, which was a wedding present from my mother, he took along with him, as he was not able to bear being parted from it.) I watched him carefully replace the bricks and then straighten his back. Poor Father, he was trying so hard not to cry!

Dear Diary,

I sat up all night watching for dawn to break over the mountains. Perhaps it is the very last time that I will see the darkness of night lift from over these snowy peaks. I feel strangely calm now. It also occurs to me that this may be the last time that I sit and write in my diary. So many 'last' things. Isn't it sad? Sometimes I think that I have imagined all this, and that tomorrow I will find myself innocently back at my school desk, giggling with my girlfriends over some lecture given by an over-stern teacher. If I ever come back and see this well beloved place again, I will look for these scribblings. I decided that I will place this diary in Father's hiding place, along with the other valuables for it, too, belongs to the past.

There is nothing anyone can do for us now except to pray for us all.

Your broken-hearted,
Ditta.

" — *and how did you find the diary again?*"
"*I returned a year later from the Gehinnom. I managed to get back to my hometown, with a cousin, and locate our house.*

Of course, everything was almost unrecognizable, but I knew exactly what I was looking for. The chimney was still intact, and I moved out the bricks in exactly the same way as I had watched Father replacing them on that very last evening. Everything was still there. I recovered a brooch that belonged to my great grandmother. These are the only 'heirlooms' I have of my youth, and I guard them fiercely. Underneath these things, where I had placed it surreptitiously that very night a year earlier, was my diary — completely untouched.

"I was moved beyond words. It was as if I had recovered a small piece of my life, when so much else had been lost. I cried when I reread it then. It was the first time I could really and truly cry since the night we left our house. Even during the worst, even in Auschwitz, I never cried properly!"

"I am not quite sure how I will tell the rest of my story, as the diary ends the night that I hid it. Nevertheless, everything, every vile thing, is etched indelibly in my mind, like this number that is burned into my flesh.

"It is so hard, so hard to retell, just like reopening an old wound. May neither of you ever know such pain.

"I will address the rest of my story to you, my dearest children, as I once, as a frightened child all those years ago, addressed my diary."

For you it is worth being in the world, continuing to breathe in and out. But there was a time when I doubted my ability to do just this. When we emerged from the *Gehinnom*, we were numb. Our hearts were turned into stone. There is a limit to loss, a limit to feeling. If one loses too much, one ceases to feel and this in itself is a *chessed*. To become part of the 'real world' again, one has to somehow allow oneself to 'feel,' to become connected to others. This is the paradox we must struggle with, day after day.

∽∾∽

That morning — yes, where were we? I had sat awake in my little sitting chair the whole night. Then, I hid my diary. That was practically the last act I carried out in my own home. In the morning, they began collecting us. We carried our bags on our shoulders, and we wore the mandatory large yellow stars on our lapels. Crowds of gentiles lined the streets to see the Jews leaving town. I heard one fellow turn to his neighbour in the crowd and remark, "There goes 'the marked brigade,'" as we passed.

It was the end of March, and the nights were still very cold. But that night we were left to sleep outside in the yard of the school building. There is a first time for everything, children, and this was the first night that I had ever in my life slept in the open. Our bodies became stiff and frozen, but more than that, it was the indignity which hurt us. It was as if we had been cast out of the company of civilized human beings. They also say that the first time is always the worst, and that afterwards one becomes more and more immune. This is true. This treatment was to be repeated many times, but it never, ever hurt me as much as on this first occasion. It also grieved me to the core to see my beloved mother and father, and my carefree brother, being made to suffer like this. Morning came and with it no respite, for now the searching began and it proceeded in alphabetical order. My mother's closest friend, who was a few rows ahead of us, simply passed out, stone cold.

"Don't let it happen to you, mother," I remember praying, "or I shall just be unable to bear it."

Our name came towards the end of the list. Well, they took all our valuables. We wanted to keep a little money with us, in case we would need it later on. So, we hid it in the door of the WC. Of course, we were taking a tremendous risk, but we were quite used to it by then. I knew most of the detectives by sight, all except the chief inspector, who was from the 'Koner,' the most terrible of torture chambers in Budapest. It was well known that no one ever emerged from there alive.

One can never measure the depths of one's endurance, and when it came to our turn I was quite cool. Even the inspector praised me. Afterwards, I obtained permission to go to the toilet and I retrieved the money. I was doing it for my family, and that gave me courage. How I endured these things I cannot really explain, but I did.

There was an old man in our group who used to be my father's teacher. (He was a learned man and quite an authority on halachic matters.) I approached him and asked, "What are the laws concerning the consumption of non-kosher food under these circumstances, and for the future?"

He pondered for a moment, then said, "Milk (dairy) dishes you may eat, should the need arise. With regard to meat," he explained, "only when it is a question of life and death. And then, only eat sparingly."

Children, you should know that I managed to keep these rulings throughout what was to come. It never constituted a real problem, as food was given to us very sparingly. But, you see that we clung to the *halachah*, to the old ways, even in our darkest hours. It was this that gave our lives some semblance of reality. Had we, G-d forbid, abandoned these things, we would have been lost. Does this seem a simplification to you? That is how things were then, everything became somehow simplified, and reduced to clearer proportions.

Where did this kind of spiritual strength come from?
It was all there in my childhood. It was a kind of reservoir,
which in the 'unspeakable world' we fell into, provided

something enduring to draw upon. I do not know if it was
possible to survive any other way — survive spiritually, I
mean, as well as physically.

What we had as children was the broad outlook typical to
Hungarian Jewry, as well as a staunch honesty in our
frumkeit. Whereas our standards in Jewish study may have
been considered basic, compared with the standard of Jewish
education for girls today, I imbibed from my parents this
unflinching attitude of non-compromise. One small incident
stands out in my mind. I was 6 years old and I had an
excruciating toothache. Instead of troubling my mother to take
me, I, with my father's knowledge, took myself off, after school,
all alone, to the dentist. Arriving home, hours later, my
mother inquired, "Who went with you?" I replied firmly:
"I was not afraid to go alone, for you see, I wasn't really alone
— I went with Hashem."

I have a recollection of that time that I ask you to commit to your memory. On the fourth day, we were told we were leaving the school yard. We were gathered together and marched off toward the station.

At the station, a non-Jewish high-school teacher was waiting for us. He had been a teacher in a lower form, but we knew him by sight. It was March, and he had pulled his somewhat shabby coat around him to keep out the wind, and had turned up his collar. He kept his hands in his pockets. He was a tall, gaunt man, and slightly stooped, the typical academic. On that particular day, he had a hollowed-out look, as if he were seeing images which would in the future haunt his every waking hour. He seemed to be scanning the crowds, looking for someone specific.

"Yossi," he called out, for it turned out he had come to say goodbye to one of his favorite young pupils.

The boy, in line with his family, turned his head to see who had called him. He recognized his teacher, and stepped toward him.

Our police escorts shouted at the boy to get back in line, but the young boy and his teacher clung to one another, oblivious to all threats.

"My dearest Yossi," his teacher said. "You are just like a son to me. Just believe that you will come back home my boy, just believe it," and the tears were running freely down both their cheeks.

At this signal all of us around them, who had managed for so long to keep back our tears, began to cry. We cried for Yossi, we cried for his teacher, we cried for ourselves.

Why I ask you to commit this particular story to your memory is to demonstrate that not everything in those days was black or white. There was great evil, but counterbalancing this, there were occasional acts of great goodness and humanity. There were those who were pleased at our departure, but equally there were others who grieved for us, who grieved for a humanity sunk so low as to perpetrate such acts. Every action has its counterpoint. Yet I often think, had there been enough 'good' of this sort to balance out the evil, the evil might never have sucked us in. The fact of the matter is, there wasn't.

We were prodded toward the trains, for all the world, like some herd of recalcitrant cattle. The trains had, by this point, come to symbolize for us something immensely sinister and evil, so that we all now had the true deep feeling that this was the end of the line for us. My father, being a Kohen, placed his hands over each of our bent, heads in turn, and recited the priestly blessing:

"May the L-rd bless you and safeguard you."

We mounted the trains. The trains began to move. But our end had not yet come. We were granted a short period of reprieve. We arrived at a larger neighboring town, where a ghetto had been constructed. Here, Jewish families took us into their homes. Who could account for this? Why were we not deported then, and only later? There is so much that to this very day remains unclear.[10]

<hr />

As I have said, we were taken in that day by a Jewish family. They were, I remember, a young couple with two small children and an elderly grandfather living with them. All in all, three families were crammed into a small, two-room flat. But I cannot describe to you what a *Gan Eden* (paradise) this was. To sleep once again in a bed, made up with clean sheets ... And in this is contained another lesson for you, my children. Repeat after me. Never take these simple, homey things for granted — a clean bed, a roof over your heads, a hot meal ...

A few days later, in the middle of the night, the sirens sounded and simultaneously there came a loud hammering on the door. We had become somewhat used to being woken in the middle of the night, and therefore slept lightly at the best of times. At first, we jumped out of bed and started dressing, ready for the bunker. But as we opened the door, we realized that this was a police raid. We were being ordered to dress quickly and get out onto the street and march. My children, I later had the misfortune to take part in many such midnight marches. But this first time, stumbling out of a confused sleep, half-dressed, huddling on the raw night street with my parents and brother, was by far the worst. No one spoke. We were all sure that this time we were being marched straight to our deaths. This was part of their infernal strategy, to wear us down with alternating false hope and despair, to paralyze us emotionally. My only hope was that, whatever it was that we were facing, it would be over soon. We stood shivering in the pouring rain in an open field

<hr />

10. We had arrived at the larger town of Satoraljaulyhely. This town had been turned into a holding depot for Jews from the surrounding region. Here we were brought, and then gradually, in the months to come, this town was emptied out. In total, four transports departed, bound for Auschwitz.

until the cold gray morning broke, a ragged mixture of humanity, the elderly, young children, tiny babies. From time to time, I scanned the faces of our guards, searching for something remotely resembling common human sympathy, but failed to find it.

This occasion proved to be nothing but another false alarm. Later, we found out that a radio had been found in a neighboring house, and that this was the pretext given for the nighttime raid. Of course, there was really no reason required. A wire fence was now erected around the ghetto, making it even smaller. We were gradually being squeezed, and squeezed further into a dry, zestless pulp. We were moved to a new location, and in our new quarters we did not have beds, so there was nothing to do but to sleep on the floor.

During those long, unsleeping hours, between nightfall and dawn, thoughts from the past resurrected themselves. I remembered, in particular, Mother's rich singing voice. It was Mother who had taught me to sing and to appreciate music. She had kindled my interest in poetry. She spoke a flawless German and was well-versed in the works of Schiller and Goethe and other German and Hungarian poets.

Now, this same Mother, so delicate and refined in nature, could not sleep because the floor was too hard. And I could not sleep, watching her.

In this confined space there were a number of families packed together. It was very important to keep the house clean on a daily basis, and much of the housework fell on me. Some of the older girls became 'nurses' in hospitals, which were packed to capacity. They gained these nursing skills by taking a first-aid course given by one of the doctors. In whatever spare time we had, we still sought to maintain social contacts. Several times, I visited my schoolteacher in the hospital. I also visited my father's teacher, whom I had asked for guidelines in *kashrus* observance when we were first deported. Sadly, they both died there, and in the midst of our own tragedy, we mourned them.

My father was in charge of the distribution of the food that we were given. This was a difficult responsibility as there was so little food to go around, but then he had always been a gifted organizer.[11] We could obtain beans, peas, potatoes and other such staple foods in moderate quantities. As I had never been a 'big eater,' I personally never experienced extreme hunger in this particular ghetto. (It must be said that conditions in other ghettos may have been much worse.)

However, our general situation was worsening. Occasionally, transports left the ghetto to unknown destinations. One day, it was the turn of our street, and our next-door neighbors were taken to the trains. This meant one thing and one thing only — we were next.

Our spirits alternately rose and fell. There were as many individual reactions to our situation as there were victims. Some young people married during this brief interlude. Their attitude was: "Live each day to the fullest" and "Eat and drink for tomorrow we die." Conversely, others committed suicide, for they saw clearly the tragic hopelessness of our position. We all knew that we were caught in a giant net. It was only a matter of time before the enemy would decide, entirely at his own convenience, to finish us off.

Of those who had been taken away on the trains, there was, of course, no word.

Children, I could not just sit and wait to be 'dragged away.' Can you understand this? A terrible fury at the helplessness of our situation built up in me, for I was young and vigorous and still

11. Food in the ghetto was not plentiful by any stretch of the imagination, but compared to what was to come in the *lagers*, technically we were not 'starving.')

thought that I could change things. I would not resign myself to this fate. I could not.

So many thoughts crowded through my brain. Oh, if only we could stretch time a little. News was reaching us daily that the Russians were not far off. If we could hang on a while, they would arrive to liberate us. But, in my more rational moments, I knew that the odds of things turning out this way were minuscule.

The word was that we would be deported the following day. It was the first mild day in early spring. I remember running out into the ghetto streets. Passersby stopped and stared at me as I ran, hot tears streaming down my face. Strangely, I did not encounter any Hungarian guards that afternoon. When I had run to the ghetto's farthest reaches, I laid my head against the ghetto fence and cried and cried until I was spent. Then I looked up at the sky and saw a pinkish-gray cloud spread itself out against the fresh spring blueness, and then a single white-winged bird silhouetted against the cloud. I thought, "Ditta, the world still contains such beauty and such freedom." In that moment, I vowed that despite everything, I would live and survive. I would bear witness to my people's suffering, the best, the tenderest and most invincible people in all the world.

How the deportees said farewell to one another, and then went to their unknown fates … How they waited for news of their loved ones … How they hoped against hope and prayed as only the condemned can … One day it would all matter — my pain and that of my family; the terror of the smallest child that whimpered as he entered that springtime's trains in his mother's arms; a single teardrop rolling down a ghetto dweller's sunken cheeks. It would not simply vanish into nothingness, like a puff of tired smoke. It must not!

I went home that afternoon and washed my face. And then, I decided on a course of action.

My story builds slowly to its crescendo or, perhaps, its lowest point, but this point has not yet been reached. We avoided death with all our cunning and yet, how it chased us. We were like pawns on a monstrous chessboard. I had decided to take some action, and as I ponder now, with the benefit of hindsight, I myself am amazed at the decisiveness of the young girl I was then. In times of great trouble, the gravity of the situation itself imposes its own laws, and with it comes a G-d-given, quite luminous clarity.

There was a certain Jewish girl from my hometown who, together with the gentile governor's grandson, was responsible for drawing up lists for the transports from our ghetto. This young man was only 20 years old, but it was he whom I would have to entreat to keep us here just a little longer, so I went to his office. His Jewish secretary was prepared to plead my case. She told him that my mother, who had only just turned 40, was ill. The boy, for that is what he was, answered: "If she is ill, let her perish." However, after some persuasion, he relented. "Here," he said, scribbling furiously on a piece of paper and then tossing it to me contemptuously. "Now get out of my office." When I finally looked at the slip of paper, I saw that it was an address. We would obviously have to move in there immediately. We were a sorry group who, dragging our meager possessions, moved into our new lodgings, this time consisting of one room. However, anything was better than being included in the transport.

The sound of Russian guns grew louder every day. In reality, we were later to learn that they were still far away, and we were only engaged in the most desperate and pathetic type of wishful thinking!

One week, then two weeks passed. Then came the, by now, expected news that a new transport was being prepared. Once more, I tried my ploy of approaching the governor's grandson, but this time it failed. It seemed as though all my cards had finally been played out.

It was at this point that it came to our attention that doctors, nurses and Jewish policemen were being allowed to stay on. I managed to procure a job as a nurse, accompanying doctors on their rounds. If only my father could become a guard, we would have a chance to stay on. But could this be arranged?

⁕⁕⁕

Children, may I, at this point, explain something quite funda-
mental about the various situations in which we found ourselves
at that fateful time. Even in the ghetto, even in the camps, there
was a certain pattern into which our daily lives fell. The common
denominators were lower, that is all. By this I mean that in the
ghetto, one's specifics were the amount of living space one had
been allotted, one's food ration, and one's work detail. In the
lager, it was how to obtain an extra ration of bread or soup, how
to survive the next selection. It is amazing how quickly one
adapted to these frameworks, however horrific. This was important, for those who failed to grasp the rules perished more quickly.

It was in this way that I knew almost instinctively that what we
needed now were 'connections.'

I went straight to our community leader who, in conjunction
with several other Jews, was in charge of appointing our own
policemen. This course of action was not as simple as it sounds. I
asked to speak to him privately, and he granted my request. I told
him that according to our information, the present police force
was leaving and a new police force was taking over. I told him
that we knew one of these police officers personally, and we
expected him to help us to escape. Alternatively, we would like
my father to be chosen as a policeman, so that we could all
remain.

The community leader said he would help us. He was true to
his word and shortly after this, Father was picked to be a policeman. His organizing capabilities were apparent even in this desperate situation, so for a few weeks, we entered a kind of lull. In
his new role, Father managed to bring us home some extras, such
as milk, eggs and butter. But things never remained stable for
long. The ghetto was now made smaller, since the third transport
had already left. We were ordered out of our old accommoda-
tion, bringing home to us the true precariousness of our situation. After much searching, we found a new room. We had to
complete our move before nightfall. As Father was on duty,

Mother very weak, and my brother too young to be of much help, mostly everything fell on my shoulders. I managed to obtain a few mattresses and after making several journeys, I was able to complete the move virtually on my own.

> "So far you had managed to avoid being deported. Did you now feel at heart that your days were numbered?"
>
> "Yes, of course. Every day that we managed to avoid deportation was a triumph. But only a temporary one, for we knew that at any moment we might be taken. We had managed to 'get around' the rules, but ultimately we knew that there were no 'rules' except those which our enemies created. They could adhere to them or change them at whim. And, of course, it was becoming tragically apparent that the ghetto would one day soon be emptied. There would now be a fourth, and last, transport, and we would undoubtedly be on it. Beyond this, we dared not think, and by this I mean the implications for our nation as a whole. Of course, we only possessed fragmented images. Anything approaching the true picture is only granted with the benefit of hindsight."

Every morning I would awake, look out of small window of our 'room,' and mentally mouth the words: "Thank you, G-d, for the fact that we are still here ..." On what would turn out to be one of our last mornings in the ghetto, a tiny sparrow flew onto our window ledge. It looked at me with a searching eye, "Share your crust with me." So I opened the window a crack, and passed out my crumbs in an honorable fashion. I thought, "If I can still share my crumbs, we are not quite done for. After all, it means that we still have what to give."

Children, it is true what they say, "The end comes when you least expect it." You anticipate the worst, with a terrible perverse longing, and then one day it just creeps up on you unawares like some shadowy thief, and knocks you to the floor.

For months and months we had been anticipating 'the end' at every moment. With every footstep in the hallway, every harsh Germanic cry, we thought: "They have come for us now ..." But now, when we were lulled into a quiet time of false security, yes, just then 'it' finally occurred.

One of the last pieces of news to reach us in the ghetto was that two of our best-known doctors and their wives had committed suicide. One of these was our own family doctor at home. Even as a young child, if I fell in the street, I would run straight to Dr. Sabo, for his ministrations brought immediate comfort. His home was an ever-open place of refuge to us in any moment of trouble. He had been one of the last Jews to be allowed to remain in Sarospotok for the Germans needed his services. When they came to deport him to the ghetto, he and his wife injected themselves with poison. On what was to prove our last evening in the ghetto, I wept tears of inconsolable grief for Dr. Sabo and his wife.

Night fell, and morning dawned. There was a knocking on our door. "Raus, raus." We were thoroughly familiar by now with the customary routine of eviction and, looking at one another silently, understood that the end had come. Now, there could be no more excuses, no more evasions, no more lies. None of these would help. We were allowed to take two sets of clothing but nothing else. Out on the street, the searching began, and also the hitting and beating with rubber truncheons. When they hit my father, I let out an almost primeval scream, for this hurt me more than when I was hit.

I knew the Hungarian policeman who was examining our bags and I whispered to him, "Don't you recognize me?"

He nodded almost imperceptibly and ceased searching our bags.

So, nothing was actually confiscated from us.

Next they stripped both men and women of their clothing. To this day, I cannot explain how, but Mother and I managed to remain fully dressed, and mingled with the crowd. We had our winter coats on and our heavy parcels on our backs. This was the middle of June and the heat was absolutely unbearable. Perspiration ran down our foreheads in never-ceasing rivulets. The guards laughingly said to us, "Chuck it all away. It will be taken from you anyhow."

How right they were, but still we clung to the slight security that our possessions afforded us. If we need 'nothing,' we will cease to be technically 'alive.' Subconsciously, I suppose that is what we felt.

We were all near collapse, physical and mental, by the time we were finally loaded onto the cattle cars. However, this proved not to be any respite, but rather an intensification of our torture. We were crammed into the trains, approximately eighty people and their luggage to a compartment. As we entered, the police continued to beat us and hassle us. Since we were the last group of Jews to leave the ghetto, the thought flitted through my mind, like a frightened starling, that no Jews remained in the whole district to be harassed and tortured. Now the wooden doors were slammed shut. Almost complete darkness reigned, for there was only a tiny barred opening to allow a pathetic dredge of daylight into the compartment.

Soon our voices ceased to rise and fall in conversation, prayer or weeping. One by one we fell silent, even infants, who had been wailing due to the confinement and lack of food. It was a deep and terrible silence which now descended on us like a pall.

It was as if the stable lineaments of the mask, which we had always thought constituted reality, had somehow been shifted drastically. Surfaces, edges, realities had all become hopelessly blurred. "What is reality – this wooden floor under our feet, this suffocating, foul darkness, our neighbor's hot breath on our cheek, this helpless descent into a seemingly, bottomless pit?"

It was late afternoon before the train finally spluttered into movement. We must have traveled about a mile or two when it stopped again. This time we were in a tunnel. I assumed that it was a new means of frightening us. We half-expected gas to be blown through the tunnel at any moment. However, this did not happen.

As night fell and the air grew cold, I fell to musing about a young policeman who had been on the platform as we left. He had shouted after me, "Hey there, you are so young and you are going to die."

I did not reply. As if goaded by my silence, he continued, "But the world is so beautiful, does it not hurt you to leave it?"

He wanted an answer. He needed an answer. But I turned my back on him sharply. Now in the blackness of the tunnel, I wanted to turn back and shout after him, "Yes, I want to live. Oh, how I want to live. But it is you who have condemned us to death."

In the utter unmitigated blackness, a rabbi began to speak in a soft voice. "My brothers and sisters. You know that it is impossible for them to kill all of us Jews. It can never happen. Many of us will perish, but there will be survivors, for our Creator has promised the Jewish people 'eternal life.'"

When he ceased speaking, there were a few strangulated sobs, then again silence. Hours passed, perhaps a whole night. When the train at last moved out of the tunnel, we saw that the day had indeed dawned.

We became stiff in our cramped seats. Sometimes an arm, sometimes a leg would become completely numbed. The nights were freezing while in the daytime it grew unbearably hot and stuffy. Our compartment was searched again at the next station and additional items confiscated by our captors. Hours, days passed in this indeterminate way.

It might have been the second or third day when the train began to rise. We saw at once that we were entering the famous Tatra mountains, the Hungarian Alps. How I had longed to visit this region as a child! One summer I had even forgone my ice cream and saved my pocket money in the hope of achieving this. Now, here I was in the landscape of my dreams, the towering green mountains with their snow-capped peaks, the sinuous rivers, the sudden, cascading waterfalls. And I was seeing it all from the inside of a train with people like living ghosts. I was seeing it with the eyes of the dead!

Here I must stop for a while, for this memory is one of the most painful to me.

～～～

"You finish by saying that this memory is especially painful for you. Can you explain why?"

"Perhaps it is that cruel inside-out feeling which we were to encounter later, too. You know, we could have been for all the world a bunch of tourists on a pleasurable sightseeing tour. The setting was right, the climate was pleasant, yet we were instead a group of condemned Jews, on our way to an unknown fate. Do you see? We were a kind of parody of our own situation. Here the irony came from the setting. Later on, it was a more conscious effect, deliberately engineered by the Germans — like the famous sign which would greet us at the entrance to Auschwitz-Birkenau: 'Arbeit Macht Frei,' the supreme irony; or the bands of heaftlinge who played classical tunes to accompany us to our work details; in fact, the lager was a parody of the world as we know it. It was a topsy-turvy world, an inverted black hole, where evil was the ruling principle. It was the antithesis of Sinai, a place from which no written or oral law was ever to emerge. An ending instead of a beginning, death-affirming instead of life-affirming, the hole of history down which the Jews, drawn from every corner of their exile, were meant to disappear — forever."

～～～

In my narrative, the nearer we approach the 'kingdom of evil,' the harder it is to continue the story. We must have felt something of this too, as the train drew nearer its destination, the presence of a great unnamed evil.

A man at my side suddenly began to act strangely. His countenance was deathly pale but he now jumped up with jerky movements, and tried to fling himself out of the car. We pulled him back and the guard shouted threateningly at him. Resigned, all the fight withdrawn from him, he sank back on the floor. In a scarcely audible monotone, he began to tell us his story:

"My wife and I lived in Poland, for she was Polish born, with our young daughter. One evening, in 1942, I returned home from work to find that my wife had disappeared. The neighbors had seen her being arrested by German police. They had dragged her away in front of our little daughter, whom they had left quite alone. My daughter and I managed to escape to Budapest where I was arrested, this time leaving my daughter in hiding. I know quite well where we are heading now, to Auschwitz. It is an extermination camp, nobody comes out of there alive. You are taken for a shower, and instead of water, gas comes out of the taps. Even if we are lucky and end up in Plazow, which is a working camp, there too, they force you to work under the most grueling conditions. I have heard that there are constant selections, and that they can kill you if you look sad, frightened, or perhaps if you permit yourself a rare smile, just as the mood strikes them."

When he had finished speaking, we all just stared at him, open-mouthed. Poor man! The double loss of his wife and infant daughter has driven him insane. Otherwise, how in the world could he visualize and describe such scenarios!?

At this, my other neighbor began to speak in a low monotone. He was an elderly, white-bearded man, so we listened to him respectfully.

"We have all sinned grievously. We have a Torah, the scroll of Moses, which sets our laws. We knew what was right and what was wrong, but we neglected these laws. Yes, we have sinned greatly and this is our punishment. Let us now go to our deaths with the A-mighty's words in our mouths."

He pronounced these words with absolute conviction. He was not attempting to be melodramatic. This was the spirit in which he intended to meet death.

Yet another fellow traveler began to sing an aria from Puccini's Tosca: "My dream of love has vanished forever, the time has flown, I die in despair! And never have I loved life so much!"

At this I felt myself ravaged with a slow tortured madness. My heart sung out: "Master of the Universe. I am only 17 years old. I have not lived yet. I had hoped to marry and have children. Is all this now to be denied to me?"

Wild thoughts flew through my head. I would burst open the cattle car with my bare hands. Why were we all simply sitting here, allowing ourselves to be neatly transported towards a probable death? I would step, bound, leap out of the constraints. I managed to pry open a crack and feel a shaft of air on my face. But the day is springlike, with a hint of breezy freedom. Oh, this criminally beautiful spring day. The guards are vigilant. They have already noticed me.

"Get down, get down. What is she doing?" they cry with one voice, as if the sight of a young girl trying to feel a little air on her face is somehow beyond belief.

But now, the train has stopped at a station. My mother manages to lean out of our wagon and ask a railway man, "Where do they take us?"

"Auschwitz."

"What will happen to us there?"

The guard raises his fingers and indicates a cut throat. The train begins to move again, gathers momentum. My mother begins to cry. Father tries to console her. He is ever the optimist, but even his optimism is beginning to fade. At long last, we pass at high speed some ragged, seemingly elderly prisoners. To us they look like gypsies, but someone shouts out that no, they are Jews and that they are alive!

We are all standing on tiptoes now, craning our necks to see this strange sight.

"They live, they live," we cry with one voice. We begin to pass miles and miles of dugouts and watchtowers. At length, the train's pace begins to slow down. This seems to be some sort of fortified city we are entering.

How we knew, I cannot explain, but knowledge there was that we were entering some kind of new domain. Was — was it, at long last, the fabled kingdom of the night?

❧

"You had arrived at Auschwitz?"

"Yes. Do you know, the name itself still makes me shudder, even after all these years. There was a sense of howling evil, of bleakness. Auschwitz — a vastness, an incomprehensibility. To step into Auschwitz was like stepping straight into our doom."

"There are those who say you could have fought back. You had superiority in numbers."

"Yes, but in every other way we were utterly helpless. You know that this familiar accusation — that we were led to our deaths like sheep — makes me want to weep. We had no weapons, we were not organized. We had undergone months, in some cases years, of ghetto life, starvation, brutalization, terror, uncertainty. And they were so clever, so diabolically clever. The concealment lasted up until the very last moment. We knew that death was their ultimate intention for us. But do you know that the gas chambers were disguised to look like shower rooms? Notices, in many European languages, exhorted the victims to hang up their clothes, tie their shoes neatly in pairs, as they would need them afterwards. It was only once inside that they realized ... Can you imagine, such a realization as this, seeing the door close behind them, and

no way out? We found out after the war, from inquiries that we made, what a difficult and unnatural death it was. Ah, but you have made me talk, and of such things as I had no wish to ..."

An arrival at a long-awaited destination usually brings relief. The discomforts of the journey are past, one anticipates rest and recovery of one's strength. Not so this arrival. Oh, how we had in the bleakest, most profound reaches of the night that was our journey, anticipated arrival at a destination, any destination, for this would bring a cessation of movement, of being confined in the overcrowded cattle cars; an end, also, to guessing our fate. Something would crystallize and become certain.

However, even these vague, cloudlike anticipations dissipated the moment the train stopped. The doors were thrust open and an immediate shouting of instructions followed. This was interspersed with the barking of trained dogs. A thousand orders, issuing from all directions, assailed us.

"Leave your parcels behind. They will be given to you later."

"Hurry, quick, quick, schnell ..."

"Raus, raus ..."

It seemed that some Polish Jews who were inmates now passed among us in their striped pajamas. They began deftly unpacking the wagon.

We bombarded them with questions.

"Can I take my toothbrush, my soap, this small bag?"

"The toothbrush is unimportant," they answered in curiously dead tones.

"But, are we going to stay alive?"

"Ah, that is the question!"

Turning to my father, another said, "You will live. But forget about your parcels."

Stepping out onto what seemed to be a giant railway siding or ramp, we saw that German officers were quickly separating the men from the women. Mother and I arrived at the SS command. I was holding her arm tightly, oh, so tightly. Ahead of us, my friend and her mother were parted. My mother whispered sadly, "I knew." But by some strange chance, Mother and I were not parted as we passed the officer in command. He left us together.[12] Then he must have realized his mistake, for we had hardly taken a few steps, when he bounded after us, pulling me back and waving my mother on ahead. I struggled. The only thing I wanted in the world was not to leave my mother's side.

"Let me be. Let me go with her," I cried.

The SS officer smiled, a polite smile, full of falsehood.

"You will see your mother tomorrow, I do assure you."

My mother looked back at me, a final glance. Never had I seen her features so distorted, so tortured and ravaged.

"What will become of you?" she shouted after me, and then … "Ditta, take care of yourself …"

This then was 'farewell,' the proverbial moment of parting, but not in a dusty station or sobbing at a bed of death. Even these were denied us. The muddy ramp, the dense sky, the strange smell of burning in our nostrils, the barking of dogs, the SS officer pulling me away … all these were with us as we turned for that final glance. A second later we were torn apart, and I, in my naiveté, had not grasped the moment for what it was. But my mother knew that we would not meet again, at least not in this earthly life.

My children, I wish for you, oh, what do I wish? Perhaps only this — that you might never know such grey, wordless farewells, such unnameable tearings apart as we experienced,

---

12. In retrospect this must have been because I was so thin and small that I looked like a very young child. It was Nazi 'policy' to send 'mothers and young children' together to their fate.

without the freedom necessary to dignify them with the title 'human loss.' Of all the denials that were heaped upon us, I think that this was the most devastating.

So, I say to you, 'feel' everything to its utmost — both joy and pain. Never allow yourselves to become numb. In the ability to 'feel,' and to exercise these feelings, lies the most valuable aspect of our doomed 'human condition.'

I must tell you, incidentally, that the SS commander who had smiled so falsely at me and assured me that I would see my mother the following day, was none other than that infamous war criminal Dr. Mengele. So, in one sense, I owed my life to him. (Later, he would select me once more for life!) I was now alone, separated from my family. I truly believed that we were all being put to work in separate parts of the camp, and that we would meet again eventually. Even when they took us for a shower, unlike some of the others, I did not think that gas would come from the taps. They took away our clothes, but left some of us our shoes. I had some kind of premonition not to wear my good ones. I was wearing an old, high, lace-up pair, and these they left me for the duration. These were far more comfortable than the pairs of wooden shoes the others were issued. The next step was the shaving of our heads, which was done with the most efficient machines. A line was left down the middle of our heads, marking us out as prisoners, and making it impossible for us to escape. Some girls had magnificent long tresses, and they fainted from the shock of being shaved. Many women survivors will cite this moment of 'shaving' as the 'moment of transformation,' from a free individual to a prisoner and *untermensch*. (To me, however, the shaving of the head was not quite so shocking, as Orthodox girls cover their heads after marriage, and normally cut their hair short.) All these preparations should have reassured us that they meant to keep us alive. But then again, one had no real way of knowing. Now, they gave us a little water to drink, but those girls who had fainted were left lying on the ground without any water. Polish Jewish women were in charge of this stage of the operation. They treated us harshly, berating us for not being 'quick' enough, for not speeding up the process. My first impression of them was they had lost their minds through so much suffering. Later, we understood they were acting under strict SS orders.

Meanwhile, we were kept standing in this 'hall of transformation' totally unclothed, with German soldiers wandering in and out of the room. We were left in this state during that whole long night. At daybreak, we were finally issued some clothing. We were directed to a pile of garments, and told to put on any of the prison uniforms. Now, catching sight of one another, our heads shaven, dressed in ill-fitting, shapeless, prison uniforms, we were virtually unrecognizable, even to our relatives or friends. Our transformation was complete. We now owned *nothing*. Everything had been taken from us, even our names. We were totally and utterly dehumanized. One girl sidled up to me and whispered, "Do you still believe that you will see your mother tomorrow?"

"Oh, yes, oh yes!" I still believed it, for I wanted to believe it.

Human resilience is endless and so is its capacity for self-delusion. I continued to 'see' my mother everywhere I looked. We were led outside and made to stand under the burning sun, but still without any food or drink (not counting the few drops of water we had been given after being shaved). I was dreadfully thirsty, and so weak. I lay down on the Auschwitz sand, which was more like a muddy dust, and like Jacob, our forefather, rested my head on some stones. As I lay there, some music started up, and this was the first time I heard this crazy, maddening, heart-gripping 'tom-tom' music that would accompany us daily on our way to work. It must have been hours later — for we had lost touch with time and reality by now — that we were taken to an empty barracks called *Lager B*. There were no beds here, and we were still without food or water. It began to rain, and we ran outside to catch the rainwater in our mouths, which cooled us down a little. But the noise we made in doing this soon drew the attention of our guards, and we were driven back into the barracks. We were told that we were on no account to leave the barracks, and that anyone who did so would be shot.

Tension mounted. Noises outside the barracks escalated. A frightful scream was heard. We rushed to the window. A woman had been running to her child. She was shot dead only yards from where the child stretched out its hand in greeting.

By now our nerves were all stretched to the breaking point. Looking out again, I saw a crowd of women being driven into the next block. Now I was sure that among them I saw my mother. I knew that there was talk of moving our group of young workers to another camp. I decided that I must go to Mother, otherwise I would be moved on and never ever see her again. In my overwrought state, I worked myself up to fever pitch.

"She needs me, poor Mother," I thought. "We need each other."

I held onto the papers with my particulars, and waited for the guard to look aside. This he never did. And then slowly, ever so slowly, came the dawning that it was all futile, my wild hopes of joining her. I would surely be shot on the spot. No, there was no escape possible, no freedom of movement, nothing.

I threw down my papers, and with them my body, onto the cold stone floor. By this time, I was kicking and screaming, my hand gripping and scratching my bald head, which I was banging onto the floor. Subconsciously I must have known that Mother had already been taken to the gas chamber, perhaps at that very moment she was taking her last, contorted breath. So what I was doing, in reality, was mourning for her. But this I did not 'know' with my conscious mind. Even the inalienable human right of mourning our dead was denied us 'down there.' Later, much later, as survivors, we would come to feel acutely this sense of having been denied the proper mourning period for our parents. Thus, I think that the sense of being 'in mourning' never really leaves us. Part of me died there that night, for when the other girls had managed to calm me, and I at last came to, there was quite simply an aching howling void — which would never again be filled.

❧

> *"You say that this loss, the loss of your parents, is a void that can never be filled. More than that, perhaps, this loss is passed on to the next generation, our generation."*
>
> *"I am coming to realize that more and more. We missed not having parents, but you missed out by not having grandparents. This is something that can never ever be redressed. Even more than that, we hoped, when we emerged from that hell, that such a holocaust would never again be allowed to happen, and that the human race would finally learn its lesson. But what do we see? An oh so similar pattern of events reoccurs in parts of Africa, in Bosnia ... It is happening before our very eyes."*

❧

Our introduction to Auschwitz and *lager* life was suitably harsh. We were left without any food for two whole days. On the train I had hardly eaten for three days, so I did not expect my strength to hold out for long. Death, I supposed, could not be far away. We slept or dozed fitfully on the stone floor. When we awoke it was only to the realization that the nightmare was real, and not the product of our overworked imaginations. When our first meal arrived, it looked as if it consisted of grass, with a few dots of carrots and some barley in it. (This, by the way, became our daily diet for the entire year spent in the *lagers*.) To top it all off, it was not kosher, and my throat tightened at each mouthful, however hungry I felt.

"This food is not fit for pigs," we would whisper to one another, and then almost simultaneously force it down our throats. We soon realized that there was no alternative. Three of us had to eat out of one dish. Now we had a change of uniform too; our clothes were changed to gray-colored shifts. That night it finally became apparent that we were not going to be kept in Auschwitz. As darkness fell, in the pouring rain, a large group of us girls were bundled into the trains, about eighty to a compartment. We were each given a slice of sausage (wurst) for the journey. But I could not eat it for it was non-kosher meat. I was holding it in my hand and squashing it this way and that, in a fit of agitation, so when the girl next to me asked for it, I gladly handed it over. She was not Jewish (her father was a priest) but she had a Jewish grandfather.

We were soaked to the skin in our gray dresses. We traveled the whole night through in this wet condition, and arrived in Cracow at noon. There had been continuous speculation as to where they were taking us, and why. We knew that there was a work camp, just outside Cracow, called Plazow. The camp was situated on the outskirts of the town. It was built over the site of the old Jewish cemetery, the main pathway to the camp being built out of the actual broken tombstones. We left the train and walked along this path, five of us in a row. We were walking on our past; the living dead, as it were, walking over our own graves.

Totally demoralized, none of us uttered a single word.

If I could compare Auschwitz with the 'lager' I was later to enter and where I was to spend many months, I would tell you that although my experience at Auschwitz was thankfully brief, it was worse, far worse than anything else we underwent.

The only way I can explain it is by saying that it was different qualitatively.

The nauseous, sickly-sweet smell, which we later knew to be 'death,' hung over the camp like a pall. It was with you every waking moment, and settled over you as you slept. We all saw the black vans, the flames, although we tried to convince ourselves that it was rubbish they were burning. The fact is that this truth was always known to us, but there is a certain safety device which will not allow one to internalize 'too' much of the truth. It is this that keeps one alive.

～～～

When we were marched into Plazow, our first impression was that of men and women hard at work building barracks. They took us to our blocks, which housed wooden bunk-beds with straw mattresses. After a time, one blanket was added for each girl, but there were three girls to one bed. Later, our rations arrived, the *lager* soup which we had tasted in Auschwitz, a small piece of bread, and an even smaller piece of margarine.

We found *lager* dwellers who had been there for some time, besides Poles, who may well have been imprisoned there for years. One of these knew my brother well, and he managed to procure a bowl for me (a most important necessity in the *lager*). The next day we were marched out to work. This was my first experience of what passed for work in these camps. We were made to carry heavy boulders up and then down again, from one place to another, from 7 in the morning until 7 at night. The rough stone surfaces tore into our still sensitive skin, creating welts and cuts almost at once. Our backs and shoulders ached unbearably. We were not allowed to stop. Anyone who paused, even for a second, felt the crack of the whip. There was no water given out during the whole day. We were supervised by kapos, who were Polish Jews, but they were watched by SS men standing behind them with their guns.

This labor, we suspected at once, had no ultimate purpose other than to torture us. The words of the Haggadah flashed through my mind: "We were slaves to Pharaoh in Egypt." We were effectively slave laborers, working at the whim of cruel taskmasters.

That night, we fell wearily onto our wooden bunks and were

soon asleep, dreaming soundlessly. "Ditta, here I have brought you some hot cocoa, to help you fall asleep." It was Mamma's voice. "Are you warm enough? Ditta, finish your homework and get some sleep. Here, I will pull up the blankets."

"Is it you, Mamma?" I could feel the touch of her delicate skin on mine, the softness of her concern. "Is it really? Stay with me, Mamma, stay." A low sound such as I had heard somewhere before. "Don't leave me, I simply cannot bear it." *Appel* — the sound of Auschwitz. "Raus, raus. Schnell. Schnell!"

"But it is still night," someone mutters. "It is only 3:30 in the morning. What do they want of us?"

"Raus, raus."

"Mamma," I turn back for a moment at the doorway of the barracks. Mamma's face splinters into the raw darkness. I whisper to her, "Mamma," but her delicate features fail to coalesce.

I lift my hand in a gesture of farewell, but find that I am waving into thin air, into nothingness ...

There was, we discovered, a pattern to life in the *lager*. That morning, 'coffee' was handed out to us. This was really mud-colored water with some sweetener in it. Then *appel*. *Appel* meant standing outside for hours in any weather conditions — rain, snow, freezing winds, burning sun — to be counted. We always stood five in a row. In the vast *appelplatz*, about 25,000 of us stood to attention each morning and night. We were a vast sea of downtrodden humanity, a disciplined mass, subdued into obeisance. We neither looked to the right nor the left. We neither smiled nor spoke. Our heads were inclined slightly downwards, as if not daring to look up at the countenances of the 'demi-gods' who ruled this gray netherworld.

Each block had a head (*lagerälteste*) who was Polish. Her second in command was a Hungarian *älteste*. The actual counting however, was done by an SS man and woman, one pair to each block.

Every evening we received our one plate of barley soup. This looked and tasted ghastly. When we first arrived we girls could hardly eat it, but later we were so famished that nothing was ever enough. We were given twenty grams of bread and, on alternate days, a double ration. Once a week, we received a little jam.

One day, as we were standing *appel,* a kapo approached us. (The kapos were generally Polish, sometimes Hungarian Jews, who supervised the workers.) He chose five girls and ordered us to go with him. Previously, when we had filled out forms, I had put down my occupation as dressmaker. We had seen some women working as dressmakers indoors and hoped that this was where they were taking us. However, when they chose ten men to join us, we became very apprehensive. Next they led us out of a large gate into a field. Here, large numbers of SS men were grouped, with enormous machine guns, ready to shoot. We were all terrified. The words of the Polish Jew on the train to Auschwitz, whom we had thought insane, came back to me in a low persistent echo: "They constantly select and kill you as they fancy."

But the Germans gave each of us a shovel and marched all fifteen of us, with our Polish *kapo,* through a second gate. Only one live-wire fence divided us from the town. We now became gardeners. If we were astonished, there was no time or energy to register this, for in *lager* life one could anticipate nothing. Sudden changes in one's situation were accepted — one learned to refrain from asking that most fundamentally human of all questions: "Why?" or "*Warum?*"

Our tasks included planting, digging, shoveling, weeding, watering, and picking fruit and vegetables. Twelve hours every day, seven days a week, usually with a half-hour break, at the most one hour. If we straightened up, even for a second, they would shout at us wildly. If we were still upright, they would hit us. It was not easy work. Our skin broke and cut easily. My index finger was cut through almost to the bone. It never had the chance to heal and the soil constantly entered the cut. Later on, when the fruit season came, we could occasionally pilfer some of the fruit we had picked

— apples, pears, red currants or gooseberries, so our job became one of the most sought after.[13] Some girls, on the other side of the fence, would cast desperate looks at us. How they longed for a piece of fresh fruit. But the SS were ever watchful, so we dared not throw them anything. Whenever possible, I would smuggle out some fruit at night. I hid them under my dress, but risked discovery and instantaneous punishment. I was fortunate, for I was so thin that they never suspected me. The knowledge that I was helping others suppressed my fear. But there were so many girls in need, and how much fruit could I take?

The fruit harvest came to an end with the summertime, and I was advised that I must find some way of earning money to buy extra food. I approached a man from our hometown, and borrowed twenty zlotys from him. When we went to work, usually young boys would come to the fence with loaves of bread to sell. I bought one bread, and then made my way to the Polish quarters. However, it was not all that easy to find customers. I wanted to make a small profit, and people had little money. Eventually, however, I managed to make some sales. I then repaid the money I had borrowed and still had a little left over. This money I would regularly hide every Shabbos under my mattress (and miraculously it was never stolen), and wait for opportunities to present themselves to supplement my rations. With these extras, I was able to help my friends. (Note: I never carried out any business transactions on Shabbos, but strangely enough lost nothing by refraining from doing so.) These opportunities only lasted for a few weeks in all. These 'extras' were a drop in the ocean for we were still starving, but contrary to popular belief, there are 'degrees' even to the most horrible suffering.

Have I given the impression that *lager* life was easy? No. The small improvements I mentioned we only managed to 'organize'

13. The fruit I picked on Shabbos, I never ate.

after weeks in Plazow had elapsed. They helped us a little to get through the day, and represented our level of 'adjustment.' At first, though, innocent and unaware, we mainly starved. What was worse, perhaps, than the starvation was the freezing cold. In those early weeks we worked on the hilltops. One image remains in my mind. It is that of myself and my friends in thin short-sleeved dresses, the wind and rain tearing us apart on that hilltop. Later, we suffered from the burning sun of summer. We were like animals left to graze in all types of weather. And would you not take pity on a poor animal, exposed to a howling gale?! However, whenever we asked ourselves the question — "How are we expected to bear this? How are we expected to work under these conditions?!" — the answer would come in all its frightfulness. "They don't care. They don't care whether we live or die. One less miserable Jew for the system to have to deal with. They simply don't care." Children — I don't expect you ever to understand this — the face of humanity was utterly turned away from us. We were left exposed, cold, comfortless, alone.

Much later, I managed to procure a warm, woolen dress from a Polish woman, but we were constantly searched as we passed through the two gates.

An incident stands out in my mind. One morning, as we stood at *appel*, an SS woman and Amon Goeth, the *commandant* of the work camp at Plazow, arrived, accompanied by several high-ranking officers. The woman was rumored to have mudered 20,000 Polish children, after having tortured them in the cruelest fashion. An elderly man was picked out for some imaginary offense and dispatched to the bunker. This meant solitary confinement, standing in a small confined place in which one was unable to turn round, without any food or water for up to forty-eight hours. Next, a girl who was discovered wearing two dresses, was made to stand in the center of the *appelplatz*, totally unclothed. The girl next to me was carrying a small bag.

"Whose is this?" she was asked.

"It is mine."

The SS woman smacked her with all her might.

"Miserable Jewess," she cried out in a murderous fury, "nothing is yours."

Next, she moved on to me. By this time, I was white and shaking, for I also had on two dresses.

"Is this a blouse?" she touched the layer of clothing beneath. I was rooted to the spot, unsure as to what reply to give, certain that something horrendous was about to happen. From the corner of my eye, I saw her incline her sleekly groomed head. One of her colleagues began to whisper something in her ear and she moved swiftly away from me. In this way, I was saved from her unpredictable wrath.

Some of the Polish women took pity on us and tried to help us in small ways. I remember one woman who put a salt-herring in my hand. We shared it among five of us. On another occasion, she gave me a cup of milk. In the *lager* this was an unimaginable treat.

We would stop at a barn before we started work each morning. There would usually be some men at work there already, reshoeing the hooves of horses belonging to German officers. The blacksmith needed open fires to heat the irons, so here was the only place we could warm up a little.

After about several months, my cousin arrived in Plazow with a new transport. How can I describe the sensation of having a relative nearby? It helped to assuage my sense of loneliness, and also, in some small way, to re-establish my identity. She knew me for who I was, and therefore I became, for those few stolen moments in her company, that person again. I was no longer a nameless number, a gray shadow in this gray underworld. She was assigned to another barracks, and I went over to see her most evenings. She had managed to keep her *siddur* with her, so that I was now able to pray from this *siddur* every night. In the mornings, while waiting in the barn, I was able to use it again. With her arrival, I visualized now clearly our mothers, who were sisters, having been put to work in another camp.

One day, I was standing for a few moments praying in this way, when I noticed a high ranking German officer coming up quietly behind me. He was in charge of our working operations.

To be found with a prayer book, prayer shawl or *tefillin* normally meant instant death. For this was a war against our spirit, as much as our bodies. He laid a hand gently on my turban where we always carried our money. I had a little cash hidden there, and he was well aware of it. But he simply gave a light laugh and left. German laughter was normally full of malice and cunning, and I shuddered at what the consequences might be. However, he seemed to have been well-meaning, for several days after this, he stopped his carriage and called me over. He filled my upturned hands with cherries. He must have been around my father's age, and suprisingly enough felt sorry for me. On another occasion, it was pouring rain. We had collected some flowers, and the girls asked me to present them to him and then to try and ask his permission to excuse us from working. He called over to our kapo, and said in a joking fashion, "Surely you cannot take them out in this downpour!"

In spite of his goodwill, I did not trust him. Some weeks later, it was again pouring, and he noticed me working in the fields. He called out to me to follow him. I was terrified. We walked silently for quite some time. At last, I broke the silence, "Where are you taking me?"

"You will see," he replied in an undertone.

By now, I was rigid with fear, my heart was literally constricted into my throat. We entered a large wooden building packed with people, who to my indescribable relief were grinding wheat into flour. He addressed me briefly, "You had better work indoors in this rain," turned smartly on his heel, and left.

"This incident is really quite remarkable."
"Yes, who can fathom the unfathomable, the German psyche? Who can delve into its innermost recesses? That same

SS officer may well have sent many Jews to their deaths. Who knows? In that world it was perfectly possible. Perhaps, he noticed in me a turn of features not unlike that of his own young daughter at home. He therefore took pity on me. To me, this small act throws into relief the greater tragedy of our fate, and makes it so much worse. You see, kindness, humanity was possible, but it was so little exercised, because on the whole they chose not to do so."

There were not many moments to lighten the gray monotony, the cold, the hunger, the fear. Thoughts of home were never far from us, and we often thought of the projected moment of our return, when all this unfathomable madness would be over. I imagined my parents and brother in the lounge of our home in Sarospotok. It would be winter, and a roaring fire would be crackling in the hearth. They would look up at once, hearing the click of the door handle.

"Well Ditta, my dear, and why have you stayed away so long? We have all missed you. Come and warm yourself. Why are you all soaked through in that strange, thin dress?!"

However, we did not communicate such thoughts to one another, we hugged them to ourselves with all the fierce determination we could muster. Yes, the homecoming would be all that we imagined, it must be so. But there was no energy to be wasted in speaking about such things, and besides, we felt a kind of inhibition in our relationships to one another. It was as if we felt, "I am So-and-so from such-and-such place. But, don't call me by my name or birthplace. Forget it. I am nothing, nobody. If I survive, we will one day meet and tell each other our names and stories. But for the moment, I am only a passing shadow in the darkness."

We felt this all the more bitterly when — bending over at our work — we would see the SS men relaxing on deck chairs in the spring sunshine with their wives and families. We were like street urchins, with our noses pressed to a rain-lashed windowpane, watching a cosy domestic scene unfolding within.

The opportunity to buy bread came to an end for a while. We now worked on a different site, planting onions and radishes. Some of the Polish Jews had managed to keep a little money with them, and some had connections on the outside, being in their own country. When I could not bear the hunger any longer, I went round to beg them for bread. I found this very difficult to do, but at times I was so weak that I felt I would faint from hunger.

However, I still retained my determination to survive. In the camp, there was a tailoring operation and one day I ventured inside. I must have looked pathetic, as I was thin and much younger looking than my age. I asked, "Please could I have some bread?"

People from all sides jumped up and gave me so many pieces of bread that I could not carry it all in my hands. When later I had the chance to buy bread again and have fruit which we had gathered, I took it straight to my cousin, who had developed scarlet fever and was in the hospital. For weeks, I managed to supply her with food and this saved her life. On one occasion, my own life was in serious danger when, in my great hunger, I ate a poisonous plant.

My children, may you never ever know such hunger which leads you to take such a desperate step. It is not the hunger which one suffers when one misses a meal. No, it is a perpetual state, which gnaws at one's innards, and allows one to think of nothing else. This is perhaps the all-pervading, soul-crushing hunger which we read about in accounts of the Destruction of the Temple. In this condition, one would eat anything. Absolutely anything.

I was ill for some days, and I thought in my delirium that I had reached the end of the road, but thank G-d, it passed.

≈≈≈

"Did you have any idea while you were held in Plazow, of the full extent of the Nazis agenda for the Jews?"

"No. Of course we had our suspicions. While in Auschwitz, we felt it to be a place of death. It was a kind of pall which hung over the place, by day and by night, and there was the smell of death in the air. In Plazow, it was different. We knew that massacres took place from time to time, on the hill. We knew, too, that any of us could be executed summarily, at the whim of Amon Goeth, or any other of the hierarchy. But — you may find this difficult to believe — we did not look too hard at what was going on around us. The struggle for survival was too intense. Having to contend with the hunger, the cold, the harshness of the work … there was not too much time for leisurely reflection."

Our group of fifteen Hungarians was guarded by a certain kapo, a Polish Jew. He was an engineer by profession, an intelligent and educated man, but what we looked upon as his 'lapses' of behavior upset us. He would tell us, without any preface, how many Jews had been, and were presently being slaughtered. We thought him cruel and heartless, and felt that he was deliberately frightening us. We continued to judge him harshly until we witnessed him being beaten up by an SS man. This SS man was placed in charge of us and he would, with no reason at all, creep up behind our kapo and beat him so fiercely that the blood woud run out of his ears, nose and mouth. After each beating, he would be black and blue, covered with bruises. Although he was young and strong, he never dared lift a finger to defend himself against the German. We began to realize why, after five years of this torture, our kapo was so unfeeling. I stopped lecturing him. One day in the pouring rain, he took off his jacket and offered it to me silently.

Our favorite job was to be chosen as housemaids, which we were once or twice. At these times, we would work in the officers' quarters, cleaning their boots and doing other lighter work. Occasionally, their wives would offer us scraps of food, somehow in the way in which one instinctively offers food to a hungry animal.

We were assigned to help gather in the wheat harvest. The men did the actual harvesting, and we had to bind the crop into sheaves. We were still unused to heavy manual tasks, and on our meager rations, harvesting was a cruelly hard task. It was midsummer, and we realized that the fast day of Tishah B'Av was approaching. Though I had been determined to fast, I was warned that this would be impossible, as I needed my strength to bring in the harvest. Rationally, I had to agree with this advice, but I prayed that I would find a way to fast as I had always done. The next day, I arrived for work with a dreadful earache. Miraculously, our kapo sent me to hide inside the haystack. We both risked being severely beaten if we were found out. I slept, warmed by the sun, until about 3 o'clock in the afternoon. When I awoke my earache had vanished and I had the energy to finish the day's work, and to complete the fast.

However often I returned to this particular memory, in later years, it never ceased to astound me, by its sheer miraculousness. The uncharacteristic laxity of the kapo, the healing power of the sun, the unprecedented opportunity to go without food, all those factors are truly inexplicable. There is still so much that we do not understand of what transpired, except that having had the 'will' to do the 'right thing,' and having taken the first step — the A-mighty gave me the ability to implement my strongly felt desire.

Another unbearable aspect of *lager* life was the systematic denial of sleep. Every morning, by 3:30 a.m., we had to stand at *appel*. The rawness of the darkness and the biting cold struck us on each occasion anew, like a well-timed blow. It seemed that our heads had barely touched the wooden bunks, when we were awoken with that fearful, low sound summoning us outside. The shouts, the barking of dogs, the relentless brightness of the searchlights, all these combined to produce a certain atmosphere of fear, which still makes my skin creep. Need we search for any more piercing contemporary vision of hell? Was this not hell itself?

On one occasion, I recall that I was so exhausted that I failed to hear our summons to the *appel*. I woke to the hiss of a German truncheon bearing down on me.

One day in that vast *appelplatz*, it was announced that the Hungarians were not diligent enough at their work. We were too soft. If we did not work harder, there would be selections, meaning that they would kill every tenth person. A certain SS man who was known to our group, approached us, and with a malicious sneer said, "Do not be afraid girls."

We answered that as we ourselves knew that we worked hard without shirking, we were not in the least afraid. However, his threats pierced us with a new fear.

Often, at night, we were forced to wait outside our barracks before we were allowed to go in to sleep. There we would sit, shivering among the Jewish tombstones which lay all around us, like jagged, decaying teeth, thin blankets about our equally thin shoulders. We must have looked, to any disinterested onlookers, had there been any, like pallid specters risen from the dead. This is an image I retain most clearly of Plazow, a camp built on the site of the old Jewish cemetery. This was a typically Germanic piece of irony, for in the 'new world order,' Jewish cemeteries were an anachronism.

Return to Auschwitz

I was still hoping against hope that I would be reunited with my family in Plazow. As each new transport arrived, I would run to make inquiries.

"Has anyone seen my father, my brother? Is there anyone by the name of Schattin in this group? Does anyone know my mother?" I scanned faces, peering into each one for perhaps I would fail to recognize them. Each time, I would turn away disappointed.

"If you want to stay alive," my friends would advise me, "forget them. Think only of yourself."

Above us on the hill stood the villa of the greatly feared SS *commandant*, Amon Goeth. He would ride out among us like a demigod on his white horse, striking a cold shaft of fear into our hearts. He would raise his gun and shoot people on sight, as the mood took him. If you smiled or looked too sad, worked too slowly or too quickly, you might bring yourself to his attention. And his attention meant one thing only — death.

Certain scenes of savagery at Plazow stand out in my mind. One day, an SS commander arrived with his lady friend. He wished to demonstrate his 'heroism' to her, so during *appel*, he summoned a Jewish prisoner whom we happened to know. He began to beat this fellow, continuing until the poor man fainted. He revived him, and then continued beating him until he was unconscious. With a graceful movement of the leg, he kicked him aside as one would a piece of debris which lay in one's path. He then kissed his lady-friend's hand, as a mark of gallantry, and like a knight who had won his joust, departed smiling.

Other 'sports' included setting enormous Alsatian dogs on us. The Germans would stand, legs akimbo, laughing heartily as we raced like the wind to get out of their path. One of my friends was bitten extremely badly.

'Beatings' were frequent and savage. One of our group of girls received a beating from a kapo in which she nearly lost her eye. Another girl's leg was cut off by the machine at which she worked. Danger and death were our constant companions, so, at times, it was not that we became unaware of them, but perhaps our level of vigilance fell ever so slightly. It was at these off-guard moments that we were most at risk.

The Polish (ever hopeful) used to console us that the Russians were nearing. Daily news reached us. The Russians are sixty, fifty, forty kilometers away.

I asked our kapo, "Do you believe now that we will be freed?"

He remained unconvinced. "They will always think of something," he said.

As it happened, he was proved right. As we were hard at work, harvesting in the fields, the news reached us that we were to be returned to Auschwitz.

The pessimists amongst us immediately predicted: "This is our end. Now they will surely dispose of us. We have done our work, and now we are not needed anymore."

Our last day in Plazow was a Shabbos. We were not marched out to work, but given orders to clean up our barracks and sew our name tags on our dresses. I remember feeling a crushing sense of sin in carrying out this chore, which was forbidden on the Sabbath. "Is it strictly necessary," I asked myself, "or can I somehow avoid doing it? Is it likely that they would check that it had been carried out?" These were the thoughts that revolved in my brain. I eventually decided to do as I was ordered, as I dared not risk any punitive action, but afterwards I still felt guilty and deeply regretted doing it.

How I longed that day to be standing silent at *appel*, wearing my uniform, though it meant being driven into the howling wind and cold. We had but one uniform, and it had to be washed, then dried under the mattress, and there was not enough time to dry it fully. How I longed for the anonymity of being marched out to walk in the fields. In that faceless labor lay our tenuous link to life. Now, we walked up and down our barracks, in ceaseless, aimless motion. We did not know what to do with ourselves; we were in limbo. As evening fell, our names were called and we were driven once more onto the trains. This time, we were *one hundred and fifty girls* to a cattle car. There was one tiny, square window covered with wire. This was our only means of gaining a little air. We traveled thus throughout two August days and nights. By day we suffocated in the heat, by night we lay shivering in the cold. We were given neither food nor water. Many of us lay in a semi-conscious stupor on the floor, with other girls simply walking over the bodies. We traveled without stopping. When at last the train's brakes ground to a halt, we realized that the rumors had been correct. We had once more been brought to that place which we had fervently prayed never again to see — Auschwitz.

> *"Would you say that this was your lowest point?"*
>
> *"It was one of my lowest points, if one can speak in this way. We lived at a level of despair which you, who pass your lives in freedom, can thankfully never know. Nevertheless, this arrival at Auschwitz, knowing now what that place meant, having undergone our initial transformation there, yes, this was a terrible shock to our already dreadfully weakened states of mind."*

We were back in Auschwitz. However hard Plazow had been, we each day had mouthed our thanks for not being in Auschwitz. This became a sort of 'additional blessing,' if you wish, to our morning litany of blessings.

At once, we underwent a swift selection. My partner and I were separated. We never knew what these divisions meant, and the underlying question — "Is this line for life or for death?" — would resound wordlessly on our lips a thousand times. Later, I learned that she had been in the line for death.

We were marched along toward the now familiar barracks. We had still been given nothing to drink, and our thirst was worse than our hunger. Our tongues clung to the roofs of our mouths, as we tottered along in giddy fashion. We caught sight of a small lake. We could see that the water was filthy and we knew that we were likely to contract typhus. But this did not prevent us from lowering our faces into the muddy liquid, and attempting to drink. Our guards shouted at us and beat us, but the sight of water had simply driven us beyond endurance.

Once again, we underwent the special Auschwitz processing, the disinfection, the shaving, being stripped of our clothing. In this condition, we were left outside during that entire night. We were still given no water. When water finally arrived at daybreak, I drank a whole can without pausing for breath. Toward morning, we were given some tattered dresses but, as usual, no underclothes. We were then taken to Birkenau, Camp B2. This turned out to be a huge barrack housing about a thousand women. If we thought 3:30 a.m. was early for *appel*, here we were awoken at 1:30. In the raw night air, we stood to attention, again in neatly formed rows of five.

Due to the soaking we had received the previous night, I caught a chill. My throat was throbbing, and my temperature soared higher and higher. We had heard rumors about sick people being sent to the crematorium, so I dared not ask for assistance. As I was walking slowly along in my dazed condition, all my limbs shaking with feverishness, our kapo, a Polish girl, pounced on me. She began beating me with her stick. I was bruised and bleeding. I had never been hit in this way before, and I began to scream. Another girl in our group walked over to me and slapped me sharply across the face. Shocked, I stopped screaming immediately. Had I not done so, I might have drawn attention to myself, which was always perilous.

The next day, we were all ordered to kneel at *appel*. But I was still shaky and fell forward. Just as I was expecting another torrent of abuses and blows to rain down on me, the kapo gave the order that we were all to roll on the sand. This was a novel punishment. I was so tired that this rolling on the sand proved to be a welcome reprieve.

The following day it poured again. Our clothes became so soaked that it was impossible to wring them out. Yet, in spite of the rain, all my symptoms simply vanished as suddenly as they had come. Yes, I say again that however hard we probe, there is much that happened 'down there' that we will never truly understand.

❧❧

> *Having come this far, I will now ask you a question. Are you not tired of listening to my account? Do the details of pain and suffering not become a little monotonous? Do they not pall? Why tell it all just as it happened? Why recount all the seemingly trivial details?*
>
> *Well, I will tell you why. In the words of the Haggadah, it is incumbent upon us to tell the story. To tell, and retell it, with all our might, all night long until every detail becomes indelibly etched in our minds.*
>
> *My story is important, but not because it is particular in any way. You could take this story and multiply it a million, six million times. It is important simply because it happened. And in this, all our stories are equally important.*
>
> *Yes, one day I stood at appel with a throbbing throat — yes, one day I was beaten — yes, I was starved and brutalized. I, Edith Shattin, an ordinary Hungarian teenager, entered the war years with her all too ordinary dreams and hopes. Why was all this taken away from us — the past, the present and the future? I wanted it back, oh, how I wanted it back! How I believed with all the fervor of youth that the long-imagined homecoming still awaited me somewhere. And, incidentally, had I not believed that, I do not believe for one moment that I would have had the will to survive.*

❧❧

My cousin who had been with me in Plazow was released from the hospital and joined us on this transport to Auschwitz.

She was such an attractive, high-spirited girl that even in this situation, her good nature shone through. I had managed to find her block, and stayed with her during the day, taking my rations with me. Once or twice I was challenged as not belonging to the block, but I was always able to hurry away on some pretext or other.

One of the girls now received a letter from an aunt. In it the aunt had written that our mothers were working together and were being treated better than we were. We drank in this consolation, this tiny glimmer of light. At times, I was glad that mother was not with us to witness our treatment, especially on the day when a friend and her mother were both badly beaten. When the mother defended her daughter, they were both made to kneel outside our barracks without food or water for a whole day.

Our bunkbeds were overloaded. Six of us slept in one small bed. If we wished to turn over, we had to call out first and then turn together. There were no mattresses. We slept on bare boards.

Here, too, the rations were more meager than in Plazow, and much of it was stolen even before it was distributed to us. We found small ways of organizing a little more, because this was vital to our survival. My cousin, for example, had a relative working in the crematorium who sent her a little food occasionally. She shared some of it with me. I also found a relative (our fathers were first cousins) who worked in the kitchen, and she sent me a little something occasionally.

One day, our arms were tattooed. The tattooing consisted of the letter 'A,' for Auschwitz, and five numbers. On average, forty to fifty pinpricks were needed to form the complete tattoo. The same needles were used for all of us, and there were no antiseptic measures taken. We soon figured out that only the healthy ones were being tattooed and that, in all probability, we would be sent out to work again.

Does it seem strange to you that although we were in Auschwitz, in the very heart of the evil, we still did not comprehend fully what was transpiring? We saw black cars transporting the sick inmates into the unknown distance. We constantly saw the flames, and smelled the peculiar smell of burning flesh. But although everyone talked of death and gas chambers, we still staunchly maintained that they were burning rubbish. Did we believe this in our heart?

Looking back, I now believe that we knew the truth all along, but that we concealed it from ourselves and from one another in order to continue to survive. "Humankind cannot bear too much reality," it has been said, and this is a truth we see borne out again and again in the course of our experiences.

A transport of Italian Jews arrived. They looked gaunt as sticks, flesh barely covering bone. They felt the cold so much that they draped their blankets around their pitiful frames. For this they were punished. Several of them had beautiful soprano voices, and in spite of their debilitated state would serenade us with "Madame Butterfly" and "Come Back to Sorrento," to keep our spirits up. They desperately wished to be tattooed. One day, however, they all disappeared.

A friend came to me with news of my father. Another girl had seen him in the next barracks. I was told to go to the fence, and someone would call him. Going to the wires was strictly forbidden, yet I was fully prepared to take the risk. For several days I approached the wire, each time with the hope of seeing my father. Each time I waited, but to no avail. On the final day, I stood waiting in my usual spot when someone approached the wire. This girl told me that an hour ago my father had left Auschwitz with a transport, destination unknown. For one of the few times since my deportation, I felt hot tears sting my cheeks and roll onto my roughly striped uniform. Father, my actual flesh-and-blood father, had been so near, and now was once again nothing but a specter to haunt my dreams. I was once more alone among strangers whose only relationship to me was that they shared all the strangeness and desperation of our common fate. I was left, to all intents and purposes, alone, crying on the other side of the fence.

That was perhaps my lowest point. There were moments when even what might now seem to us as 'trivial losses' set me teetering from my precarious balance of sanity. One day, for example, I recognized one of my dresses, worn by a kapo. A girl remarked to me, "Oh, with a red belt and navy shoes, it must have looked smart." Utterly dejected I answered, "Yes that is exactly how I always used to wear it." For in a sudden cruel flash, what I had actually seen was my former self, and then seen that self brutally thrust from my grasp just as surely as the navy dress was receding from my field of vision.

But, counterbalancing this, there were little gains too.

For example, we were always short of water and one day someone gave me a small jar. I was thrilled, for I would be able to keep a little extra water in it. However, water was not such a simple matter to obtain, as it was a long walk to the water tap and it was often locked or out of bounds. I also could not refuse girls who asked me to get a drink for them.

One evening, I met a young girl who looked no more than 14. She was crying bitterly. It took me a long time to ascertain the reason. She was terribly thirsty and could not get any water. My own tears had by now dried on my cheeks, and I offered to try for her.

"It is impossible," she said. "Everything is shut for the night."

It needed all my courage and initiative, but after some time I managed to procure a little water for her. At this, her bright blue eyes lit up through her tears and I resolved to forget all my own hardships!

How can you, children, understand this? You will think us aliens from another planet. We were. A little extra water was like manna in the desert of Auschwitz. I for one will never forget these little things, for they were the substance of what we had become. We licked the last drop of soup from the bottom of the barrel in which our food was brought; we were

glad to swallow raw potatoes. I was nearly caught because of the miserable piece of cabbage I took from the kitchen! All these are part of the story. No, they are the very fabric of the story.

〰〰

After one month in Auschwitz, we were again dispatched onto the trains. By now we knew what to expect, but then again, mounting the cattle cars at any time was not easy. Of one thing we were certain and this gladdened our hearts a little — with each turn of the wheels, we were moving further from Auschwitz.

In the car, in the heat and stench, we dozed fitfully. My thoughts returned to their familiar theme — what of my parents? How are they bearing up under the strain of the work? How can my 15-year-old brother work so hard?

The train ground to a halt. By now, we were past caring to which version of hell we had been brought. Our reception was the familiar one — SS men with truncheons and huge Alsatian dogs.

The camp itself, we soon ascertained, was situated on the outskirts of Leipzig. It had formerly been a holiday resort. Apparently, we were to be employed in an airplane factory, manufacturing parts. It was a small camp consisting in all of about five hundred women. The chosen leader of the group was a woman from my hometown. She was the same age as my mother, and her daughter had become our kapo. These two women were very generous. They were often given a whole barrel of soup and they shared it with the girls from their own hometown. Fearing that this would not last, and starved as we were, we often ate too much and developed severe stomach cramps.

Our rations were also better than in Auschwitz. We were given one third of a loaf of bread with a small piece of margarine and one piece of sausage daily. (The sausage, however, I staunchly refused to eat.)

We were given instructions about the work we would be expected to do in the factory, but we were not yet put to work. In this interim period, we had to keep the large halls, our quarters and the gardens in order.

After several weeks in this camp, I developed an infection on my leg. This had started while I was in Auschwitz and over the weeks it had become gradually worse. The so-called camp doctor gave me a cream to rub onto it, but this was the wrong treatment. After a while, I could hardly stand on my leg. The walk to the factory and back and having to stand at work were becoming virtually impossible. My friends urged me to eat the sausage, as they suspected that the infection had flared up due to a total lack of protein. They convinced me that every morsel of food would help. Strangely enough, one night, lying on my hard bunk bed, I dreamed that my uncle Yaakov Deutsch, a well known rabbi, appeared to me. He advised me to eat the sausage, as it was a clear case of 'danger to life.' This I did, and the infection began to subside.

We were working nights, and were allowed to sleep during the day, but the sirens would often wake us. We were gladdened to hear these sounds, as it meant that the war was drawing to a close. Yet, we were afraid, too, of the ever-present danger of falling bombs. Fortunately, our camp remained intact.

Winter came and we had no coats. We later found out that the camp *commandant* had commandeered our winter coats the moment we stepped off the trains. He kept them piled up in a storeroom during that severe winter. We were also not given any underwear. When liberation drew near, he would try to ingratiate himself to us, stating that he had always tried to treat us 'like a father' (his phrase). We had to stand for *appel* in the freezing wind, for hours. We washed ourselves daily in the cold, open washrooms, with ice-cold water, to toughen us, thereby enabling us to survive. In the factory, we worked long hours. Four of us were assigned to one machine, producing the same part. Our supervisor praised me for learning the job fast; I managed to produce one hundred and ten parts per day. When the supervisor had left the shop floor, we would try to mix faulty parts with good ones. We had no wish to help Germany in its war effort.

In this camp, some of us had managed to keep a calendar, and many girls had *siddurim*. This meant that we knew exactly when Shabbos and other festivals fell. On Yom Kippur, we Orthodox girls begged the others to fast. I gave my ration to the only girl who said she was unable to fast. On Pesach, I sold my bread for potatoes (to a resistance worker), and for the first two days, I lived on these only. During the remaining six days, I had soup but no bread. These were extremely difficult measures to carry through, but I was determined to attempt not to eat *chometz* during this period. After Pesach, the resistance worker gave me two breads. He was very decent. I hoarded this bread and, as you will see, this saved my life.

Friday nights were spent indulging in the old longings for home. I would lie on the wooden bunk and shut my eyes. If I concentrated sufficiently, I could be home, dozing in front of the fire, serving the special chestnut cake which my mother used to bake for the long wintry Friday nights. I dared not open my eyes, for I knew that reality would intrude at once. Then my fanciful dreams of home would dissipate like so much snow at the first touch of spring.

"Your story is drawing to its close."
"Yes, and we sensed this all around us — not only in the sirens and the sounds of bombs falling and guns booming in the distance, but also in the attitude of the SS. This was a more subtle change, and only those who had long been under their subjugation could divine it. We prisoners knew it ... We sensed it ... The cracks in the edifice were beginning to appear ... The writing was on the wall."

The bombings increased daily, and we heard the frequent boom of guns. The SS men and women were growing daily more nervous. It was something ever so subtle — a change in their attitude, which had formerly been, "You will never be free. We will rule over you forever." There was now a certain droop of the shoulders, an insinuation in the once arrogant gesture, which seemed to be suggesting, "One day the unthinkable might happen, and everything will return to how it was before. Then you and I will be on equal footing. Judge us leniently." Of course, this was never said openly in just these words, but it was a feeling that hung in the air — like the promise of spring.

The last day in the factory was one which I shall never forget. The sirens sounded, and we were sent to the bunker — a massively built area underneath the factory. Suddenly, it felt as though the whole bunker was being lifted into the air. The lights went out, we were in complete blackness, and then came the most deafening blast I have ever experienced. It soon became apparent that we had suffered a direct hit. Emerging from the bunker, we realized that there was no factory above us. Germans were being carried away on stretchers. We found it hard to believe that we had actually survived.

Events began to move quickly after this. My older friend, who was possessed of a keen insight, warned us that 'the end' would not come in a simple way. It would probably, she said, be the most gruesome of all our experiences.

The camp commandant summoned the whole camp to *appel,* and began to speak.

"You know, of course, from the bombings and explosions, that the front line is very near. In a few moments, the governors of the factory will assume responsibility for your welfare until you can return to your families. I have to go away, but remember, I was always good to you, like a father in fact. Speak kindly of me."

His blue eyes shifted nervously. For the first time, he met our eyes, seeking some sign of assent in them. But we remained impassive. More speeches followed by representatives of the factory. The next instant, the SS commander was called away. We waited, but for what? We waited because we had been trained to stand and wait for orders. But he did not return. Fear knotted our stomachs, as the biting wind tore around us. At last, an order was passed down.

"Everybody pack. We depart at 3 p.m."

～～

The end of my story is nearing. My older, more experienced friend, was right. In some ways we were still to experience the worst. And always, with the tantalizing sensation that we were a stone's throw from freedom.

We were given some provisions for our impending journey, a little bread, one carrot, a little margarine. We were urged into formations of five, the familiar grouping. Thus, we began to walk. In the end, we simply walked, for seventeen days and seventeen nights. It seemed that the whole SS force was guarding us. Despite this, one or two of my friends managed to escape. I heard them whispering one or two rows behind me, then they quietly dropped their belongings and disappeared into the thickly brooding dark forest on either side of us.

We walked without stopping, right through the night. At daybreak we were counted. When each day it was discovered how many girls had escaped, the commander phoned through orders for their arrests.

After a short rest and a plate of soup, we were again driven to our feet. From all directions we could hear the sounds of fierce battles underway, the sound of gunshots, and heavier, pounding weapons. The Germans told us that we were now on our way to a new camp. That night was the most terrifying of all. We were left to sleep outside in a field. It was a cold April night, and it was raining. As our heads touched the cold earth, the air attack began. Bombs and grenades were splintering and falling all about us. Surrounded as we were by the retreating German army, we were shaking with a terrible fear. Again, we were led through a dark overgrown forest, and during the day that followed we encountered several Jewish transports, just like our own. Their captors were shooting at them, and we heard shots followed by the most horrific, ear-splitting screams.

My friends on my row turned to one another and said: "This is the end. They mean to do this to us, too. Let us escape now."

I argued with them. I pointed out that with our shaven heads, our tattooed arms, our prison uniforms, we would not have the slightest chance of remaining at large. However, my arguments were to no avail and, at a certain signal, they dropped behind and were swallowed up into the dense night almost immediately. By morning, however, they were recaptured. Bedraggled and totally demoralized, they were driven back into line by the SS, with a torrent of verbal and physical abuse. The next morning, we were given nothing to eat. We collected grass and boiled it. By this time, we were fearfully weak. We also picked raw potatoes and ate them, despite SS warnings that if we were caught doing this we would be shot. Corpses littered the roadside as we walked. They must have been the remains of earlier transports. At our next stop, some boiled potatoes were distributed. Debilitated and starving as we were, there was a tremendous fight for them. Suddenly, our SS commander pulled out his gun and ordered us all to line up. The barrel of his gun was pointing at me, no more than two feet from where I stood. He was roaring like a maddened lion, threatening to exterminate us all. It was only the exhortations of his wife that he might soon have to face Allied justice, that calmed him down. Slowly, ever so slowly, he dropped his gun and ordered us to march.

As we walked, we were ordered to leave behind those that were ill and unable to continue. I remember thinking that we were leaving them behind like unwanted litter. We felt their blank, staring eyes bore into our retreating backs. A-mighty G-d, I prayed, let their end be swift and merciful. Do not allow them to suffer too long.

One girl had her *siddur* with her, and we prayed together in a low undertone. When she was left behind, unable to continue, we continued to pray by heart. If the words were jumbled, we prayed to G-d to decipher them on our behalf, for only He knew what lay in our hearts, heavy as stones in a river of unwept tears.

Time passed, but we had lost track of time. Time became for us the heavy tread of our wooden clogs on the damp earth as we drove onwards like automatons. "Don't think, just march, step forward then forward again." Time became nothing but day turning into night, and then to the tread of our feet, into day again. Time was this endless hobnailed march, with mud on its boots, as we walked no longer with our feet, but willed on only by our slowly numbing brains. We walked ourselves into sleep, and then into wakening. We walked on into mountains, into thick snow, and we lay on the snow and woke half-frozen to walk again. Sometimes, we walked without food, sometimes we walked on air, and into thin air. Can one die standing up? Yes, we could easily then have walked from sleep into death, that place of greater peace where there were no more live wires, no more watchtowers, no more selections or roughly barked orders, no more hunger, tiredness, aching limbs, raw blisters. We walked ourselves into nothingness — and then, it seemed into the great beyond.

We arrived in Dresden to find a burned-out shell of a city. The streets were deserted, and people were afraid to open their doors to us when we went to beg for a little bread. (Until that point we had kept from starvation by eating the two loaves of bread given to me after Pesach by that blessed resistance worker.) In some places they set their dogs on us, but in others we were lucky, for while searching in the rubbish bins we found carrot and kohlrabi peels. The inhabitants themselves had little to eat.

We could hardly walk. I remember a certain house where we knocked and they gave us each a piece of bread with some pasty substance on it. This is another image which will be engraved in my memory — a group of us standing at a gate, with tears pouring, unchecked, down our cheeks. These were tears partially of relief because we had been given a whole piece of bread to eat, and also tears of shame, for we realized that we had sunk so low as to beg for it.

That day we had to run to rejoin our transport which was just leaving. The SS truncheons were in motion again, hassling and hurrying us onward and upward. Now we were forced to ascend a slippery mountainside. The ground was muddy and we constantly fell back. But we had to carry on, for we were afraid of receiving further beatings. We clung to branches for a more secure hold, for all the world like survivors of a great shipwreck clinging to driftwood. The branches tore at our arms and legs, our blood mingling freely with the mud below. By nightfall, we had reached a school, and this was the only night we spent indoors. I removed my soaking wet clothes and hung them up to dry. However, I shivered the whole night through. In the morning, the clothes were still damp.

The next day we arrived at another town. By now, my shoes were falling apart. My feet were bleeding and covered with sores, and I was dragging one leg after another. When a German woman saw me, she cried out, "I will send you some shoes." This she did, and along with it two apples. Apart from the physical relief this act afforded, it also acted as a balm to our tired spirits. Not all Germans then were evil, and wished only to see us dead. There remained, in some of them at least, a spark of basic humanity, of human decency.

This was to be our last night on the road. After seventeen days and nights of marching, we arrived at a barn. Here, the girls simply trampled over one another in an effort to find somewhere to lay their heads, walking over hands, heads and legs. As I finally descended into the realm of fitful sleep, Mamma appeared to me. Her pale, delicate features coalesced quietly in the darkness. She looked so alive, so real. But there was a terrible unnamed sadness in her eyes. I reached out to touch her, fingering her porcelain skin gently, as I had been accustomed to do as a child. I meant to tell her not to fret so, but she began to speak in a low voice, "Ditta, my child, all will be well with you. Tomorrow you shall be free. Unfortunately, we will not meet again."

I awoke to tears coursing down my haggard cheeks.

"Mamma, mamma," I cried out, "I do not want to be free without you."

The next day, we walked into Theresienstadt, where we were later liberated by the Russians, and handed over to the Red Cross. There our torturers were finally driven back.

"Mamma, you were right, though others refused to believe it. We had walked our way to freedom."

❧❧

"It must have seemed quite unbelievable to you that you were finally free."

"Yes, it was — still is — unbelievable. I do not think that we have ever really taken it in. Everything is so much more meaningful to us — a proper bath, a clean bed, having enough to eat, reading a book. It seems that we will never be able to take these 'little' things, which constitute a normal life, for granted again. Perhaps, perhaps after all, this is the only blessing to have come out of those years."

"But in other ways the adjustment to a free life was difficult?"

"Yes, and it was weeks later, after strenuous inquiries, that I finally realized, like thousands of others, that there was no homecoming to be reenacted. They were all gone, sucked into a catastrophe of immense proportions. How could this have happened? Relatives, neighbors, communities, a whole way of life — gone, vanished, transmuted into ashes. And while we had labored, keeping body and soul together, this other 'thing' — which we could scarcely understand — had been happening. The 'smell of burning,' the sickly sweet stench of Auschwitz, recurred in our nostrils. It was 'we' they were burning all along! Tears are not enough, monuments are not

*enough, memorials, meetings, words — nothing, nothing will
ever compensate for this. What, what have you lost? An entire
nation? Nobody has ever heard of such a loss. It is
incomprehensible. Yet, our nation lived on … I say this to
you, but can you understand this?"*

"The missing pieces of my childhood? Yes."

*"So, let me address you children once more, to attempt to
complete my story, for what it is worth."*

So the story continues — after freedom and alongside freedom.
How close we were, even at the end, to annihilation we only discovered afterwards. The Germans had planned to murder all the
inmates of the camp of Theresienstadt, into which we had walked
on that Spring day in 1945, in the gas chambers. But two German
engineers went over to the Russians to save their own skins, so the
Russians entered earlier than had originally been intended, and we
were saved.

As we had walked towards the town of Theresienstadt, on our
way to the camp, we had passed through an orchard. The branches
of the trees swayed softly in the caressing spring breezes, weighted
down with the full-throated flowering of pale pink and white blos-
soms. This sight caught at my thin throat with a convulsive grip. All
this gentle beauty — from which we had been cut off for so long!

On the streets, people were jumping for joy. Large Russian cars
and tanks passed us, hooting and honking playfully, soldiers leaning over, throwing sweets, chocolates, and cigarettes. The soldiers
who stepped out of their cars were lifted high in the air by the few
remaining healthy Jewish men. We all cheered them on.

Life in Theresienstadt continued after liberation, in haphazard,
almost nomadic manner. One of our first concerns was to try to
assuage our terrible, growing pangs of hunger. We could quite easily dispose of a loaf of bread in one sitting. One day, I managed to
fry about forty pancakes on an open fire. The gray, gritty smoke

made my eyes stream with tears, but the effort was thoroughly appreciated. What we craved more then anything, though, was 'sweet food.' So, one morning our group went to town. We met others along the way, and someone asked me my age. "So young," this older woman exclaimed, "you have your whole life in front of you. How I wish I were still a teenager!" For the first time in months, perhaps years, on this glorious May morning, I felt that there may be a tinge of truth in this cliché.

The shops we found had been looted, and lay open to the street, like jagged teeth. Anyone could just walk in and take whatever he picked up. People went home with wireless radio sets, record players, and all sorts of valuables, but we were not 'looters' in any sense of the word.

I only took a jar of jam and some fruit salad, mainly to build up my strength. I did not have the heart to take anything else. We were to make one more outing in the coming weeks. Not all of our walks produced the same joyous feelings as this first one, for we would see bodies strewn by the side of streets. They had been hastily covered with rough blankets, and then simply left. On another occasion, we knocked at a house and tried to enter it. The door was opened by a former SS soldier who pointed his shotgun at us. He seemed to be just as terrified of us as we were of him, so after a pause of a few moments, we left without the food for which we were searching.

In town, we heard that fighting continued in the mountains as some of the German forces refused to surrender. There were other dangers too, in these first, perilous days of freedom. One day, we were on our way back from town, as it grew dark. We would have had to pass through a Russian army camp, so we decided that the lesser of two evils would be to hitchhike. A car containing a couple of Russian officers stopped for us. As we girls more than doubled their number, we decided to accept their offer. We arrived at our camp safely, having refused their offer to go to their hotel for a bag full of chocolate.

One of the greatest dangers we faced was that of overeating, for our stomachs were so shrunken that terrible results could, and did, ensue. In liberated Theresienstadt, hundreds continued to drop like flies in those first days of 'freedom.' This situation was the same in all the liberated camps.

Most evenings, in what had been the *appelplatz*, the inhabitants of the camp gathered. Besides the English and Russian national, practically every nationality was represented — Hungarians, Germans, Poles, Greeks, Czechs, Dutch, Danish, Belgian, French and Austrian. I went to the *appelplatz* mainly in the hope of meeting somebody who could tell me about my family.

One night, I did meet someone who told me that he had heard rumors that my father had still been alive in February. However, this information subsequently proved to be unreliable. As night succeeded night, this faint hope, too, ebbed silently away. Now, only one wish remained to me — to return home.

In truth, my story is all but over. At long last, I have told you what has been locked in my heart for so long, and you have heard your father's story. After the war was over, in a land foreign to both of us, we met and married. Your father once said, "The scars will be with us forever, outside and in." I have said that our struggle continued long after our freedom was finally granted, and so it was. First, there was the struggle to accommodate ourselves to the terrible growing awareness that there was no family to go back to. All over Europe, survivors were crawling out of the ashes to this very realization. In addition, we suffered both day and night from stomach cramps, as our systems were too debilitated to absorb the food we were now being offered. Our physical states were so weak that thousands died in the terrible aftermath of the destruction.

Days, weeks, passed in a strange limbo-like state. We were free, but we had yet to grasp what we were supposed to do with this so-called freedom.

As the weeks went by, the force that impelled me homeward, a force which I did not fully comprehend, did not abate. My journey home began by mounting the train again. This was a terrible moment for me; however, I forced myself to remember that I was no longer being pulled towards my death. We were traveling towards a location of our own choice.

The wheels of the train ground on inexorably. With a start, I sprang out of my reverie. I realized that the Sabbath was nearing. "I am free now." I repeated the words to myself, as though they were a magic formula. "Therefore, I should not knowingly break the Sabbath." So I alighted and walked toward the nearest town. This proved to be a long walk of several miles. There I met a large group of young people who had returned from the camps a short while beforehand. We spent an uplifting Shabbos together. Traveling to the next town, I met up with some cousins. One of them had been my camp partner in Plazow. They broke the news, as gently as they were able to, that none of my family had returned. Our mothers had been gassed. I had survived the cataclysm, but the sole hope which had sustained me through the months of torment — the projected reunion with my family — lay crushed underfoot like so much gray rubble. I heard the words, I listened to them patiently. I believed them there and then and I cried bitterly. I was thankful that I was not alone to face this heartbreaking news.

It was a summer morning when I made my way from the train station to our house. I was with my cousin, who, anxious for my welfare, had offered to accompany me. Once again, I saw the familiar backdrop of mountains, the streets which I had thought never again to see. As we drew nearer to my street, it was obvious that it was still much as I remembered it. Could it be possible? Could everything have remained the same? Finally, the house itself. Hand on the doorknob, I enter, with nothing left to lose but my dreams. The house had not been bombed, true, but it had been ransacked by soldiers, Russians or Romanians, in transit. Heaps of rubbish lay everywhere, piles of photos, household items, clothing. I stood almost immobilized not knowing where to look.

This was when, in a sudden fever of remembering, I uncovered the hiding place in the chimney. My hand trembled as I searched for the exact place. Let the things be there, let something of us remain when all else has been despoiled. And in my mind's-eye, I was transported back to the mountains of personal possessions that I had been told had been stored in the 'Canada' section of Auschwitz. I saw the photographs, the treasured mementos, the child's stuffed toy, the trinkets from home. But you cannot destroy lives utterly without trace, I thought. Something always remains. That was their mistake.

My hands move deftly now.

"Yes, yes," I turn to my cousin "The things are there ... Look, look, here is my grandmother's brooch, and the diary in which I wrote up to the very day we left ..."

Although my cousin eyes the things rather indifferently, I am animated now. It is as if among the obvious ruins of my childhood, I have re-established who I am.

I stayed some weeks longer in our hometown. I felt that I had unfinished business to conclude. One part of the "unfinished business" included recovering the *Sefer Torah,* which my father had given away into the 'safekeeping' of the 'policeman.' My cousin and I managed to locate it — and to bring it home! The *Sefer Torah* itself, which had been in our family for years, was intact — but the valuable 'silver ornaments' had mysteriously disappeared. We took the Torah to the shul, where it was the only one.

I was also by now in desperate need of money. So I rented our house, after it had been cleaned up sufficiently, but only received one month's rent, no more.

All the goods in our shop had been auctioned in our absence. A deep anger and frustration welled up in me, as I thought of the years of toil father had invested in this shop. Nobody had the right simply to 'sell off his life.' Legally, it was very difficult to get back the remaining provisions unless, of course, I received information. The men who took the bulk of the goods from our shop were also the same people who had ransacked our house. I managed to enlist the help of several policemen, some of whom had once been employed behind the counter in our shop, and were very willing to help. We went to a certain house and found one of our crystal chandeliers. All the goods I managed to identify as belonging to the house or the shop I took to the police station.

Eventually, the case came to trial. I represented myself, and recovered every single item.

Looking back, all my bleakest frustrations went into my defense. Inflation was sky high, so the amount of money I received for the sale of these items was negligible. But, in some small way, as I left the courtroom in Sarospotok, I felt vindicated. Can you understand this?

⨂⨂⨂

The waiting was not yet over. It would take nearly a year to receive a 'visa' to the country that eventually would be my new home, England. I was spiritually sick of Hungary, my so-called 'homeland,' country of my youth, in which all that I had most cared for in the world was now lost to me.

In this no-man's land period of waiting, one event of a hopeful and joyous nature stood out like a beacon of light on a wintry day. My cousin, my camp partner, who had accompanied me back to Sarospotok, became engaged and invited me to her wedding. She had relocated to Czechoslovakia; however, shortly before the date fixed for the wedding, the Czech government changed their monetary system and all border crossing to this country were suddenly closed. I was therefore unable to receive permission to travel. However, I was not yet ready to admit defeat. I decided to go to the Hungarian side of the small bridge which marked the border. Here, I waited for several hours, until nightfall. Then, summoning up the last vestiges of my courage, I approached the customs officer. I explained, cajoled, argued that I could not possibly be a spy, finally rolling up my sleeve to reveal my tattoo. Something about me must have touched him — who knows — as he wordlessly waved me on.

My problems were not yet over, for I boarded a train, entirely without papers or money. Here, however, my unbelievable luck held out, as I met a group of Jewish girls, all heading for the same destination, and they bought a ticket for me.

My cousin was a most radiant bride, and in spite of the profound sadness of not having parents present, this wedding represented a watershed, for it proved that it was possible — like timid shoots pushing their way gently through spring soil — to make new beginnings.

~~~

The year 1946 found me in Budapest, sitting on the balcony of my relative's house. Queen Vilma Street was renowned as one of the most attractive in the city, and now it appeared at its best. Acacia trees lined both sides of the broad street, and the flowers were in full bloom. Patches of crimson, damson, and yellow assailed the eye, and the air was heavily scented. All this beauty should have infused me with a sense of tranquility, I suppose, but instead, I felt restless, uncertain of the future. My father's cousins had offered me temporary shelter until my visa arrived. They were quite exceptional people. Each of them had lost partners in the war, except their older sister, a university professor in America, married to the son of the world-famous professor Albert Einstein. However, they were not Orthodox, so that meant that I could not take my meals with them, and had to undertake a long walk and bus journey to the Joint hostel, where free meals

Edith Reifer's mother (left) with her sisters and brother. None of them survived.

were available to refugees. The days I did not manage to go there, I ate only bread and pears, which was all I could afford.

I now proceeded to put all my energies into obtaining a Russian permit. I went and spoke to the prime minister, who in turn sent me to the leader of the Communist party. I spent days in the waiting room of the embassy. Eventually, in my desperation, I passed a letter to the head of the embassy as he left the building! In the letter I wrote that I had lost all my family in the camps, including not merely my parents and younger brother, but also uncles and aunts. In England, I had cousins, among them one couple who did not have children, and they were anxiously awaiting my arrival. My mother's fervent hope had been that, should anything happen to her and my father, I should go to London. After the head of the embassy read this letter, I received promises from him and others in influential positions that I would soon obtain the necessary permit. But how the waiting tired my already jaded soul!

It ended with a telephone call assuring me that what I had long hoped for, had, in fact occurred — my Russian permit to leave Hungary had been granted. Finally, I was free to depart for England.

After leaving my cousin's home on Queen Vilma Street, I stayed for two weeks in a Red Cross transit camp. Here, determined to keep 'kosher' as I always had, I had to be content with dry provisions. However, when the leader of the camp informed me that I could begin my journey to London on the coming Friday morning, I asked if it could be delayed, as I did not want to travel on the Sabbath. After promising to inquire on my behalf, he returned with this ultimatum, "Travel tomorrow, or you will be returned to Hungary. There is simply no choice."

On Friday morning I boarded the train and began saying *Tehillim*, begging for a miracle so I would not have to travel on Shabbos. Within minutes of starting out, the train ground to a halt. We were informed that the train was making an overnight stop, and were directed to a Red Cross hostel to spend the night before resuming our journey on

Shabbos morning.

I quickly took my passport and tickets to the stationmaster and asked him when the next train was due after Shabbos. He replied, "On Tuesday." I asked, "Can I use my ticket on it?" and he answered, "Yes!" I happily returned to the Red Cross hostel and spent three extra nights there.

My journey had been paid for from London, and since I was forbidden to carry any money I was unable to buy food. After a long walk on Sunday I came to a 'Joint' kitchen, where I gratefully

Rabbi Dr. Eli Munk

received my first warm meal in two weeks. (The 'Joint' organization, established and sponsored mainly by Americans [bless them for it], deserves our heartfelt appreciation and gratitude for always being there in our time of need.) On Monday I obtained a parcel of provisions from a nearer place, and it was clear that Heavenly help was constantly assisting me.

On Tuesday I resumed my journey to Paris. Thereafter, conditions were more civilized. I went to a restaurant and then to a hotel overnight, finally reaching my destination in London the next day. My cousin, Rabbi Dr. Eli Munk (his wife Hilda was the daughter of Chief Rabbi Dr. S. Spitzer of Hamburg, my Uncle), met me at the train station.

My children, this effectively is the 'end' of my wartime experiences, and the beginning of a new chapter. But nothing in life is ever completely distinct — this is something else that one learns through experience. The boundaries between states of being are blurred — it is hard to tell where one thing begins and another ends.

Where did imprisonment end and liberation begin?

〰〰

> *"What exactly do you mean by that statement. Could you elaborate?"*
>
> *"Yes — the rest is by way of explanation, as they say.*
>
> *"When I came to England, you see, I was alone. And that sense of aloneness has never truly left me, even though I was taken in by kindly, well-meaning relatives. I think this was because before the 'catastrophe,' I had been a member of a well-established family. In this respect your father's experiences and my own coincide! I had only to travel to another town and mention my surname, for someone to immediately identify my three uncles, well-known rabbis, or my grandfather. Now, I was effectively a 'non-identity,' a refugee without a past. It was this sense of being a 'nobody' which pierced me to the core. You see, our loss was so total, so incomprehensible."*

Do you know, I sometimes think, my children, that the world was somehow 'embarrassed' by us. We ought not to have survived and borne witness to something that was so much beyond belief! "Leave us alone, let us be ... Go back to your ghosts, we do not want to be troubled with tales of gas chambers and piles of corpses. Leave us alone." We are their conscience, you see, the conscience of the world — for it was ultimately 'people' who allowed it to happen.

After the war they locked up the governors from each town without any reason and kept them in prison for months without a trail. Our governor became an old and broken man. I know because I went to his eventual trial to defend him. I spoke up for him, described how he had helped us, had done no harm to anyone and was a fine man. They freed him but the damage was done to his health. How unjust the world can be!

For myself, I have learned much along this harshest of life's paths. Lines of the Hungarian poem, "I Have Learned," often used to revolve in my head during my incarceration. This was a poem which was extremely popular, and which, as a youngster, I was often called upon to recite. Picture me, my children, the harsh wind and rain of Auschwitz or Plazow whipping at my thin gray dress, lifting heavy boulders from here to there and back again, and all the time, talking to myself: "Ditta, remember, remember those words. Repeat them, those simple, good words of homespun wisdom, until they become engraved on your soul."

> *I have learned never to be afraid of anyone*
> *Nor to judge others harshly ...*
> *I have learned to have an unshakeable belief*
> *Because without faith, life grows unbearable ...*
> *That the darkest hour of the night, rays of light can filter through ...*
> *And shedding tears is all in vain.*
> *And I have learned how vastly important it is,*
> *What we are given to help us on our way.*
> *And in life we can achieve everything*
> *We actually set our hearts and souls on,*
> *But unfortunately, almost always too late.*
> *And I have learned that however often we stumble*
> *Our G-d is always with us ...*
> *And if we fall and it hurts,*
> *The answer is that*
> *The next bruise will be less painful.*
> *And nothing is really important,*
> *Neither love, nor fame, nor glory, nor beauty,*
> *Neither great riches nor empty pockets,*
> *Not easy journeyings nor mountains of obstacles,*
> *Nor dreams, yearnings or sufferings,*
> *Nor incurable wounds, forever stinging.*
> *Only one thing truly matters*
> *In rain and storm*
> *In deed and word ...*
> *What is inside, what is inside of us ...*

My hope is that in having told my story, you will understand who we are and what we have tried to be. And finally, I say to you my children, bear in mind that above all we have tried to give you what was hardest of all to give — normality. We tried to be everything for you and to compensate for what we could not be, for the continuum which had been broken. Sometimes, I think that we aimed too high.

But how far we have actually succeeded in this aim, it is ultimately for you and you alone to judge.

Afterthought

Well, I had requested to hear my parents' story, but in their opening up the 'book' of their minds, it was as if an unpredictable genie had been conjured from a bottle. While there was so much here that I had anticipated, the stories seemed also to have a surprising elasticity and life of their own, branching out into unsought alley-ways, unexpected detours.

Although I began by expecting vast differences in my parents' stories, I could see now that both of their stories were essentially and disastrously the same, just as all Holocaust stories are part of the 'lager' story, like atoms in a molecule. However, in the manner in which they chose to tell their stories, these stories became refracted into the singularity of their lives. It was in this way that a degree of individuality could be achieved from the incomprehensible mass of suffering. Isn't it only when we say, "Yes, such and such happened to me, I experienced it I survived it," that we can begin to make sense of it at the only level which ultimately matters – the individual, human level!

They had given us something, too, of immeasurable value, forged in that most unimaginably searing of crucibles. This was apparent in their resolve, in their obstinacy, in their quite simply having clawed their way back out of hell, one painful rung at a time. This, in the simplest of facts, in having established a home, beginning anew in an alien land, which constituted the most death-defying of statements, "You tried to blow us off the face of the earth but here we are, we breathe in and out, we walk about freely, we exemplify the eternal Jew

*at his most baffling and awe inspiring." All this, despite the
scars which — in their own words — will always remain.*

⁕⁕⁕

*It is a spring morning in London, but still with the bite of
winter in it. I am preparing to go out on an errand. Father is
busy inspecting some of the rare books which he collects, and
which also form part of his business ventures. He handles the
book with a practiced hand and a well-trained eye. I think to
myself, destiny has blown him further than he ever dreamed
from the timber yard in Chrzanow. Yes, he has built for
himself a new life and it is only now that I fully understand
just how much courage was required to do this.*

*Father senses me watching him. We talk a little of this or that,
and as is his way, he makes some philosophical remark about the
nature of life. As I pull on my coat, he concludes by saying, "You
know, it is a dangerous and ruthless world out there. Go
carefully, my son, and with the A-mighty's help ..." Of course,
he means this in a general as well as a particular sense.*

*I nod absentmindedly in assent, as I have always done since
childhood, and let out the most imperceptible of sighs.*

*Mother enters the room. I think — I imagine mother as a
young girl of 14, in Sarospotok, writing in her diary,
chronicling all her pain and bewilderment, because she had no
one else to tell it to who would not be hurt too much. Will
anything ever compensate her losses? I see them now for what
they truly are, the loss of ink-stained girlhood, the loss of
sweet apple-blossom dreams, the loss of youth itself.*

"You are going out?"

I reply in the affirmative.

"Well, be successful (zei matzliach)," she says cheerfully.

I turn to go.

"Oh, and one more thing ..."

"Yes mother?"

"Come back to us safely, with the A-mighty's help."

AN ALBUM
OF
SURVIVAL

The extended family of Leibel Reifer, before the war

The wedding of Yitzchok Reifer

Reb Shmuel and Edith Reifer

Avrohom Reifer, 1 year old

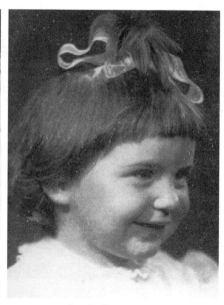

Sara Reifer, 2 ½ years

At the wedding of Sara Reifer to Hershel Frydenson

Avrohom Reifer and his wife Rivka

Avrohom Reifer with his wife and children

The children of Avrohom Reifer

This volume is part of
THE ARTSCROLL SERIES®
an ongoing project of
translations, commentaries and expositions
on Scripture, Mishnah, Talmud, Halachah,
liturgy, history, the classic Rabbinic writings,
biographies and thought.

For a brochure of current publications
visit your local Hebrew bookseller
or contact the publisher:

Mesorah Publications, ltd

4401 Second Avenue
Brooklyn, New York 11232
(718) 921-9000
www.artscroll.com